Guidance notes and flow charts for the

Engineering and Construction Short Contract

The NEC3 Engineering and Construction Short Contract is an alternative to
NEC3 Engineering and Construction Contract and is for use with contracts
which do not require sophisticated management techniques,
comprise straightforward work and impose only low risks on
both the Employer and the Contractor

An NEC document

June 2005

NEC is a division of Thomas Telford Ltd, which is a wholly owned subsidiary of the Institution of Civil Engineers (ICE), the owner and developer of the NEC.

The NEC is a family of standard contracts, each of which has these characteristics:

- Its use stimulates good management of the relationship between the two parties to the contract and, hence, of the work included in the contract.
- It can be used in a wide variety of commercial situations, for a wide variety of types of work and in any location.
- It is a clear and simple document – using language and a structure which are straightforward and easily understood.

These guidance notes and flow charts are for the Engineering and Construction Short Contract and the Engineering and Construction Short Subcontract, which are both part of the NEC family and are consistent with all other NEC3 documents.

ISBN (complete box set) 978 07277 3675 8
ISBN (this document) 978 07277 3373 3
ISBN (Engineering and Construction Short Contract) 978 07277 3372 6

First edition 1999
Second edition June 2005
Reprinted 2007, 2010, 2011, 2012

Cover photo, Golden Jubilee Bridge, courtesy of City of Westminster

9 8 7 6 5 4 3

British Library Cataloguing in Publication Data for this publication is available from the British Library.

Typeset by Academic + Technical, Bristol

Printed and bound in Great Britain by Bell & Bain Limited, Glasgow, UK

CONTENTS

ACKNOWLEDGEMENTS

The first edition of the NEC Engineering and Construction Short Contract was produced by the Institution of Civil Engineers through its NEC Panel. It was mainly drafted by Dr Martin Barnes, Tom Nicholson and Nigel Shaw based on work by Andrew Baird with the assistance of Peter Higgins and advice from Professor Phillip Capper of Masons Solicitors and David Maidment of Willis Corroon Construction Risks Ltd. Contributions were also made by Ross Hayes and Jon Broome of the University of Birmingham.

For the second edition of the NEC Engineering and Construction Short Contract these guidance notes were mainly drafted by J. G. Perry, with the assistance of members of the NEC Panel. The Flow Charts were produced by Robert Gerrard and Ross Hayes with assistance from Tom Nicholson.

The original NEC was designed and drafted by Dr Martin Barnes then of Coopers and Lybrand with the assistance of Professor J. G. Perry then of the University of Birmingham, T. W. Weddell then of Travers Morgan Management, T. H. Nicholson, Consultant to the Institution of Civil Engineers, A. Norman then of the University of Manchester Institute of Science and Technology and P. A. Baird, then Corporate Contracts Consultant, Eskom, South Africa.

The members of the NEC Panel are:

    P. Higgins, BSc, CEng, FICE, FCIArb (Chairman)
    P. A. Baird, BSc, CEng, FICE, M(SA)ICE, MAPM
    M. Barnes, BSc(Eng), PhD, FREng, FICE, FCIOB, CCMI, ACIArb, MBCS, FInstCES, FAPM
    A. J. Bates, FRICS, MInstCES
    A. J. M. Blackler, BA, LLB(Cantab), MCIArb
    P. T. Cousins, BEng(Tech), DipArb, CEng, MICE, MCIArb, MCMI
    L. T. Eames, BSc, FRICS, FCIOB
    F. Forward, BA(Hons), DipArch, MSc(Const Law), RIBA, FCIArb
    Professor J. G. Perry, MEng, PhD, CEng, FICE, MAPM
    N. C. Shaw, FCIPS, CEng, MIMechE
    T. W. Weddell, BSc, CEng, DIC, FICE, FIStructE, ACIArb

NEC Consultant:

    R. A. Gerrard, BSc(Hons), MRICS, FCIArb, FInstCES

Secretariat:

    A. Cole, LLB, LLM, BL
    J. M. Hawkins, BA(Hons), MSc
    F. N. Vernon (Technical Adviser), BSc, CEng, MICE

INTRODUCTION

| **The notes in boxes like this one** | printed within the NEC Engineering and Construction Short Contract (ECSC), explain how to complete the ECSC when it is used for a simple, low risk contract. These boxed notes are reproduced in these guidance notes, which also explain the background to the ECSC and give guidance for its use as a main contract. Supplementary guidance is also given on the NEC Engineering and Construction Short Subcontract (ECSS). The flow charts show the procedural logic on which the ECSC is based and are published in this volume for reference.

In these guidance notes, as in the contract itself, terms which are defined in the ECSC have capital initials and those which are identified in the Contract Data are in italics. The guidance notes and the flow charts are not part of the ECSC and have no legal function.

WHEN TO USE THE ECSC

Within the NEC family, the ECSC is the alternative to the Engineering and Construction Contract (ECC) and is for use with contracts which

- do not require sophisticated management techniques,
- comprise straightforward work and
- impose only low risks on both the *Employer* and the *Contractor*.

Users choosing between the ECSC and the ECC should base their choice purely on the level of complexity of the work required and the level of risk to each of the Parties.

THE ECSC PACKAGE

The ECSC package includes the conditions of contract and forms which, when filled in, make up a complete contract. The forms are on pages 1 to 9 of the package and are provided for

- the title page and
- Contract Data, which includes
  - The *Contractor*'s Offer,
  - The *Employer*'s Acceptance,
  - Price List,
  - Works Information and
  - Site Information.

Examples, using a fictitious small building job, are appended to these notes to illustrate how the title page, Contract Data, The *Contractor*'s Offer and The *Employer*'s Acceptance should be filled in at each of the following three stages leading to a contract.

Stage A: How an *Employer* invites tenders for a job

The *Employer* uses the package to invite tenders for proposed *works* by providing the following information on the forms and sending the package to tenderers with the invitation to tender.

- **The title page (page 1) – see example A1**
- **Contract Data (pages 2 & 3) – see example A2**
- **The *Contractor*'s Offer and the *Employer*'s Acceptance (page 4) – leave blank**
- **Price List (page 5) – see notes on subclause 50.3**

> Entries in the first four columns in this Price List are made either by the *Employer* or the tenderer.
>
> If the *Contractor* is to be paid an amount for the item which is not adjusted if the quantity of work in the item changes, the tenderer enters the amount in the Price column only; the Unit, Quantity and Rate columns being left blank.
>
> If the *Contractor* is to be paid an amount for the item of work which is the rate for the work multiplied by the quantity completed, the tenderer enters the rate which is then multiplied by the expected quantity to produce the Price, which is also entered.

- **Works Information (pages 6–8) (see notes on subclauses 11.2(13) and 60.1(1))**

> The Works Information should be a complete and precise statement of the *Employer*'s requirements. If it is incomplete or imprecise there is a risk that the *Contractor* will interpret it differently from the *Employer*'s intention. Information provided by the *Contractor* should be listed in the Works Information only if the *Employer* is satisfied that it is required, is part of a complete statement of the *Employer*'s requirements and is consistent with the other parts of the Works Information.

1 Description of the *works*

> Give a detailed description of what the *Contractor* is required to do and of any work the *Contractor* is to design.

2 Drawings

> List the drawings applicable to this contract.

3 Specifications

> List the specifications that apply to this contract.

It is important that these are thoroughly prepared and comprehensive because the ECSC definition of a Defect (subclause 11.2(3)) is based entirely on the Works Information. Include in the specifications details of

- quality standards for design (if any) and construction,
- any tests and testing procedures required and
- any specific Equipment and methods of construction to be used.

4 Constraints on how the *Contractor* Provides the Works

> State any constraints on the sequence and timing of work and on the methods and conduct of work including the requirements for any work by the *Employer*.

Refer to any specific constraints relating to the country where the *site* is. These may include provisions such as a labour intensive approach using appropriate technology, and maximising local employment.

The *Contractor* should be allowed to subcontract work without any limit (subclause 21.1). However, the *Employer* may wish to limit the extent of subcontracting if, for example, the *Contractor* is being selected for a particular expertise. The *Employer* may also wish to provide lists of subcontractors and suppliers who would be acceptable for specific categories of work or supplies. Any such constraints should be stated here.

If the *Contractor*'s work needs to be co-ordinated with other activities or contracts before Completion, define the parts of the *works* affected and state the dates by which each is to be completed.

If the *Contractor*'s work is to be affected by work done by the *Employer*, the nature of the *Employer*'s work, including the timing should be stated. This needs careful thought because, if the *Employer* does not work within the conditions stated, compensation event 60.1(5) will apply.

5 Requirements for the programme

> State whether a programme is required and, if it is, state what form it is to be in, what information is to be shown on it, when it is to be submitted and when it is to be updated.
>
> State what the use of the *works* is intended to be at their Completion as defined in subclause 11.2(1).

The programme may take the form of a list of dates, a bar chart or a network diagram, etc.

The information to be shown on the programme should include at least

- the *starting date*,
- the Completion Date,
- the *Contractor*'s planned Completion,
- key dates for the *Employer* to provide 'services and other things' (not earlier than the dates stated in part 6 of the Works Information) and
- key dates for co-ordination with other contracts (see part 4 above).

If there is anything unusual about the *Employer*'s intended use of the *works* after Completion, state in the description of the *works* (part 1 above) what the intended use is to be. For example, selling or leasing to other people or passing on to a later stage of construction (subclause 11.2(1)).

6 Services and other things provided by the *Employer*

> Describe what the *Employer* will provide such as services (including water and electricity) and 'free issue' Plant and Materials and equipment.

The descriptions should include the capacities available and the location of connection points.

If the *Employer* wants any materials from excavation and demolition to become the property of the *Contractor* they should be listed here (see notes on subclause 70.2).

- **Site Information (page 9) – see note on subclause 11.2(12) and note on subclauses 60.1(9) & 60.2**

> Give information about the *site* such as the ground conditions and any other information which is likely to affect the *Contractor*'s work such as limitations on access and the position of adjacent structures.

The information on ground conditions should include references to publicly available information relevant to the *Contractor*'s work (subclause 60.2) and information about underground or otherwise concealed services which would not be apparent from a visual inspection of the *site*.

- **Invitation to tender**

The *Employer*'s invitation to tender should include a list of suggested adjudicators from which the tenderers are asked to choose one (see notes on subclause 93.2).

The invitation to tender may also include other matters, for example

- any constraints on how the Price List should be used for the submission of tenders,
- if the *Employer* requires tenderers to give names and details of supervisory staff, Equipment to be used and methods of construction, the information should be requested in the invitation to tender (normally, it should be stated that any such details should not form part of the contract and are provided for information only),
- in some circumstances the *Employer* may also wish to draw the attention of tenderers to local employment legislation and health and safety legislation and may also emphasise the importance of gender equality (equal opportunities, equal pay for work of equal value), minimum age of employment and protection of wages (to ensure wages are paid on time and in cash).

Stage B: How a tenderer makes an offer

A tenderer uses the package to make an offer by providing information on the following forms.

- Price List (page 5) – see notes under Stage A and on subclause 50.3
- The *Contractor*'s Offer (page 4) – see example B1

> Enter the total of the Prices from the Price List.

The tenderer's covering letter should also include

- the tenderer's choice of adjudicator from the list suggested by the *Employer* or, if none is acceptable, the tenderer's own suggestions,
- any extra Works Information proposed by the tenderer and
- any additional information asked for by the *Employer* in the invitation to tender, such as
  - names and particulars of tenderer's supervisory staff or workforce proposed and
  - proposals for Equipment to be used.

The letter should also make it clear if any part of the *Contractor*'s Offer does not comply with the Contract Data or the Works Information provided by the *Employer*.

Stage C: How a contract is made

The package becomes the complete contract document when the *Employer* makes the following additional entries and sends a copy to the *Contractor* who has made the chosen offer.

- The *Employer*'s Acceptance of the offer (page 4) – see example C1.
- The title page (page 1) – *Contractor*'s name added – see example C2.
- Contract Data (page 2) – *Adjudicator*'s name added – see example C3.

Under the law of England and Wales, the contract between the *Employer* and the *Contractor* is then made. There may be other requirements in other jurisdictions.

The ECSC uses a simple offer (The *Contractor*'s Offer, page 4) and acceptance (The *Employer*'s Acceptance, page 4) to create a contract. It is emphasised that this is the most efficient and clear way of creating a simple contract and users should aim to achieve this. However, if

- the tenderer's covering letter requires changes to the documents (other than to incorporate the addition of the accepted *Adjudicator*) or
- the Employer has issued supplements to the invitation to tender amending the documents,

these need to be recorded with the *Contractor*'s Offer or the *Employer*'s Acceptance.

This is achieved either by

- the tenderer adding after the offered total of the Prices

  'This offer includes our covering letter Reference . . . . Dated . . . .' or

- the *Employer* adding into the *Employer*'s Acceptance before the signature

  'The Offer includes the information provided in . . . .'.

(This is either the tenderer's covering letter if not already mentioned in the *Contractor*'s Offer or a document or summary agreed by the two parties after the tender was received.)

NOTES ON THE CLAUSES

1 General

Actions 10

10.1   This clause obliges the *Employer* and the *Contractor* to do everything which the contract states each of them does. It is the only clause which uses the future tense. For simplicity, everything else is in the present tense.

The requirement that the Parties act 'in a spirit of mutual trust and co-operation' is in accordance with a recommendation of Sir Michael Latham in his report on the UK construction industry ('Constructing the Team', July 1994).

Identified and defined terms 11

11.1   The Contract Data is used to complete the contract by identifying terms in italics and providing the information that certain clauses state is in the Contract Data (see examples A2, B1 and C3).

11.2   The meanings of all defined terms are given in this clause.

11.2(1)   In order to have a clear definition of Completion for a particular job, the *Employer*'s intended use of the completed *works* needs to be clear. If there is any doubt, the *Employer* needs to state in the Works Information what that intention is. (See notes on Works Information part 5 under 'Stage A: How an *Employer* invites tenders for a job'.)

11.2(2)   The Completion Date is the date by which the *Contractor* is required to achieve Completion (subclauses 11.2(1) and 30.1). At the start of a contract it is stated in the Contract Data as the *completion date* but it may be changed as a result of a compensation event (subclauses 62.1 and 63.4).

11.2(3)   Defects Certificate/*defects date* – see notes on cls. 40 and 41 and on Works Information part 3 under 'Stage A: How an *Employer* invites tenders for a job' and example A2.

11.2(5)   Defined Cost is defined in this clause in terms of payments made by the *Contractor*. The term is used in the assessment of the cost effect of a compensation event (see notes on subclauses 63.2 and 63.3).

Allowable payments do not include recoverable tax. This is added when the *Contractor* is paid the Price for Work Done to Date under subclause 50.3. Otherwise, all payments made for a resource should be included subject to subclause 63.3. For example, payments for people should include payments made for them (e.g. in the United Kingdom, National Insurance contributions and PAYE payments to the Inland Revenue) as well as payments made directly to them.

11.2(6)   Equipment includes construction plant, vehicles, consumables, tools, temporary works, scaffolding, cabins and other site facilities provided by the *Contractor*, none of which are to be included in the *works*.

11.2(8)   Plant and Materials will be part of the *works* as described in the Works Information and does not include 'Equipment'.

11.2(9)   The Price for Work Done to Date (see notes on clause 50).

11.2(10)   The Prices (see notes on clause 50).

11.2(11) One use of this definition of 'Provide the Works' in conjunction with 'Works Information' (11.2(13)) is to establish the *Contractor*'s main obligation in subclause 20.1.

11.2(12) The Site Information is provided by the *Employer* and should include all the information the *Employer* has about the *site* and its surroundings which is relevant to Providing the Works (see notes on Site Information under 'Stage A: How an *Employer* invites tenders for a job' and on subclauses 60.1(9) and 60.2).

11.2(13) The Works Information is the *Employer*'s statement of what the *Contractor* is required to do in Providing the Works and what constraints the *Contractor* must comply with (subclause 20.1). The Works Information provided with the invitation to tender will be the basis of the *Contractor*'s tender and must be as comprehensive as possible (see notes on Works Information under 'Stage A: How an *Employer* invites tenders for a job'). The *Employer* may instruct a change to the Works Information during the course of a contract; this may then be a compensation event (subclause 60.1(1)).

Law **12** Orally agreed changes to the contract have no effect unless they are followed up by the procedures stated in this clause.

Communications **13**
13.2 The *period for reply*, stated by the *Employer* in the Contract Data (example A2), aims to achieve a timely turn round of communications. Its length depends on the circumstances of the job but would normally be two or three weeks. Other periods for specific actions are stated in the relevant clauses (e.g. subclause 62.1 – submission of quotations for compensation events). All such periods can be changed only by agreement between the Parties.

The *Employer*'s authority and delegation **14**
14.2 Only the *Employer*, or an authorised delegate of the *Employer* (subclause 14.4), can change the Works Information.

14.4 Some Employers may wish to delegate many of their actions from the start of the contract, for example to an architect for small building works. If this is the case, the instructions to tenderers should state who the delegate is and which actions are to be delegated.

Access to the *site* and provision of services **15**
15.1 The extent of the *site* and the *Contractor*'s access to it will normally be defined on a site layout drawing (example A2) and identified in the Site Information.

15.2 Refer to notes on Works Information part 6 under 'Stage A: How an *Employer* invites tenders for a job'.

Early warning **16**
16.1 The obligation which this clause requires of both Parties is intended to bring into the open as early as possible any matter which could adversely affect the successful outcome of the contract. Both Parties should give early warning in order to maximise the time available for taking avoiding action. If the *Employer* decides that the *Contractor* could have given early warning of a matter which results in a compensation event but did not, and has notified the *Contractor* of that decision, the sanction stated in subclause 63.5 applies.

Note that the intention of the meeting is to solve the problem. It is not to decide responsibility, or who will pay for actions taken; the relevant provisions of the contract will cover these aspects quite adequately.

2 The *Contractor*'s main responsibilities

Providing the Works **20**

20.1   This clause demonstrates the importance of thoroughly prepared and comprehensive Works Information (see notes on Works Information under 'Stage A: How an *Employer* invites tenders for a job').

20.2   The *Employer*'s acceptance of the *Contractor*'s design does not change the *Contractor*'s responsibility for it (subclause 14.3). This clause enables the *Employer* to review the design for its compliance with the Works Information and point out any unacceptable features before it is used for construction or installation.

Subcontracting and people **21**

21.1 &   As in other NEC contracts, the ECSC does not provide for nominated
21.2   subcontractors. The *Contractor* has full responsibility for Providing the Works, whether subcontracted or not (see notes on Works Information part 4 under 'Stage A: How an *Employer* invites tenders for a job').

3 Time

Starting and Completion **30**

30.1   The *starting date* has several uses in the ECSC

- it is the earliest date on which the *Contractor* can start work on the contract,
- it determines when there is an *assessment day* for payments (subclause 50.1),
- it is the start of the total period used in the assessment of an adverse weather compensation event (subclause 60.1(10)) and
- it is the start of the period during which insurance cover is required (subclause 82.1).

Refer also to notes on subclauses 11.2(1) and (2), definitions of 'Completion' and 'Completion Date' respectively.

30.2   The purpose of this clause is to keep the *Employer* up to date about the *Contractor*'s forecast date of Completion.

30.3   Before deciding the date of Completion, the *Employer* needs to check that the requirements of the definition of Completion in subclause 11.2(1) have been satisfied. (See notes on Works Information part 5 under 'Stage A: How an *Employer* invites tenders for a job' and on subclause 11.2(1).)

30.4   An *Employer*'s instruction to stop or not to start work may result in a compensation event (subclause 60.1(4)).

The programme **31**

31.1   The *Employer*'s requirements for the *Contractor*'s programme should be stated in the Works Information (see notes on Works Information part 5 under 'Stage A: How an *Employer* invites tenders for a job').

4 Defects

Searching for and notifying Defects **40**

The definition of a Defect (subclause 11.2(3)) is based entirely on the Works Information. If the *Employer* is not satisfied with work for a reason other than that it is not in accordance with the Works Information the work would not be a Defect. In order to 'correct' the work, the *Employer* would need to instruct a change to such Works Information, which would be a compensation event (subclause 60.1(1)).

The Works Information in the contract should therefore include a comprehensive specification of the standards to be achieved in the Plant and Materials and in the constructed *works*. If the *Employer* has specific requirements for inspection and testing, these should also be stated in the Works Information, including the associated procedures and responsibilities for carrying out the tests (see notes on Works Information part 3 under 'Stage A: How an *Employer* invites tenders for a job').

Where payment for work on its completion is dependent on a test being successful (see definition of Price for Work Done to Date in subclause 11.2(9)), the description of the item in the Price List should include a reference to the test stated in the Works Information. Where appropriate, separate items may be included in the Price List for carrying out tests which are the *Contractor*'s responsibility.

40.1 If no Defect is found in a search instructed by the *Employer*, a compensation event would occur (subclause 60.1(8)).

40.2 The *defects date* is fixed by a period after Completion stated by the *Employer* in the Contract Data (example A2). The length of the period will depend on the type of work and its 'settling down' characteristics but it is recommended that it is not less than twenty-six weeks.

Correcting Defects **41**

41.1 The periods for the notification and correction of Defects are illustrated in Diagram 1. Before Completion, the *Contractor* is motivated to correct all Defects which might delay Completion (subclause 11.2(1)).

41.2 The requirements for the programme may state key dates for co-ordination with other contracts or other activities by the *Employer*. A notified Defect which would prevent such work must be corrected before the key date occurs.

41.3 The *defect correction period* comes into operation after Completion to ensure the timely correction of any Defects which are outstanding or are notified after Completion and before the *defects date*. The length of the *defect correction period* is stated by the *Employer* in the Contract Data and should take account of the type of work, the *Employer*'s urgency for Defect correction and the ease of access after Completion. It would not normally be more than four weeks.

41.4 The Defects Certificate, defined in subclause 11.2(4), is issued by the *Employer* and records the state of affairs when the *Contractor*'s obligation to correct Defects ceases under the contract (although the *Contractor*'s liability for them may continue under the applicable law).

Uncorrected Defects **42**

42.1 This clause applies to any notified Defect outstanding after its *defect correction period*. This will finally include any Defect listed by the *Employer* on the Defects Certificate.

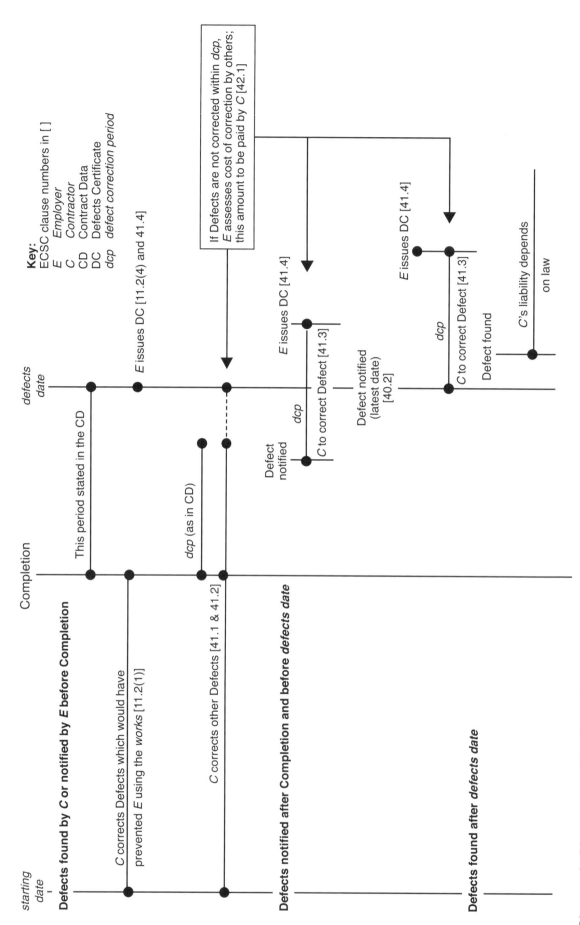

Key:
ECSC clause numbers in [ ]
E   Employer
C   Contractor
CD Contract Data
DC Defects Certificate
dcp defect correction period

If Defects are not corrected within *dcp*, *E* assesses cost of correction by others; this amount to be paid by *C* [42.1]

E issues DC [11.2(4) and 41.4]

E issues DC [41.4]

E issues DC [41.4]

C to correct Defect [41.3]

C to correct Defect [41.3]

Defect found

C's liability depends on law

Defect notified

Defect notified (latest date) [40.2]

dcp

dcp

defects date

This period stated in the CD

dcp (as in CD)

Completion

Defects found by C or notified by E before Completion

C corrects Defects which would have prevented *E* using the *works* [11.2(1)]

C corrects other Defects [41.1 & 41.2]

Defects notified after Completion and before *defects date*

starting date

Defects found after *defects date*

Diagram 1. Diagram on notification and correction of Defects.

Repairs 43

43.1 This is a general obligation on the *Contractor* to replace loss and repair damage regardless of how these may have been caused. A compensation event may occur as a result (subclause 60.1(14)).

5 Payment

Assessing the amount due 50

50.1 The *Employer*'s statement in the Contract Data fixes an *assessment day* in each month from the *starting date* until the month after the Defects Certificate has been issued (see example A2). This provides for a monthly assessment by the *Contractor* even when the amount due may be nil (e.g. after Completion).

50.2 The *Contractor* assesses the amount due by each *assessment day* and uses the assessment to apply to the *Employer* for payment.

50.3 The payment mechanism is based on the use of the Price List and two key defined and related terms – the Prices and the Price for Work Done to Date (PWDD).

- **The Price List** included in the contract provides the pricing information needed for assessing the PWDD. Notes on how to use the Price List form are included under its heading in the ECSC and are repeated in these notes under 'Stage A: How an *Employer* invites tenders for a job'.
- **The Prices** are defined in subclause 11.2(10). The second sentence of the definition provides for the pricing of those items for which a quantity and a rate are stated in the Price List.
- **The Price for Work Done to Date (PWDD)** is defined in subclause 11.2(9) and is the main component of the amount due assessed by the *Contractor* by each *assessment day*. Payments for an item in the Price List do not become due until the work described in the item has been completed unless a quantity and a rate are stated in the Price List for the item, in which case only the Price for the quantity of work completed is included.

These definitions and the layout of the Price List provide for flexibility in tendering methods including items which

a) the *Employer* describes and for which the tenderer quotes a Price,

b) the *Employer* describes with a quantity and for which the tenderer quotes a rate extended to a Price (adjustable to quantity completed),

c) the *Employer* describes and the tenderer breaks down into sub-items comprising a mixture of a) and b), each of which the tenderer quotes for,

d) the *Employer* describes and the tenderer quotes for a list of the activities necessary to complete the item, each with a Price or

e) the tenderer describes and quotes Prices or rates in accordance with the notes at the head of the Price List and the invitation to tender.

The *Employer* should include in the invitation to tender any constraints on how the Price List should be used for the submission of tenders.

It is important that item descriptions are carefully written with appropriate references to the Works Information, including testing requirements (see notes on clause 40). For measured items, the work to be covered by the rate must be clearly stated. If there is a risk of differing interpretations on how an item is measured, the method of measurement should be stated in the item description of the Price List.

The second and third bullets in subclause 50.3 state the other amounts to be added to or deducted from the PWDD to calculate the amount due. These amounts may include damages, retentions and any VAT or sales tax. It is recommended that the Parties should agree, at the start of the contract, how the administration of sales tax documentation should be dealt with as part of the payment procedure.

No provision is made for inflation. In some countries where inflation is high the *Employer* may wish to take the risk of Price increases beyond a predetermined threshold. This could be provided for in additional conditions of contract adding to the provisions of subclause 50.3.

No provision has been made for advanced payments. If the *Employer* is prepared to make an advanced payment, a separate item should be included in the Price List. The item must describe how the advanced payment is repaid.

50.4   This clause should be read in conjunction with subclause 51.2 with respect to late payments.

50.5   The *delay damages* to be stated in the Contract Data (see example A2) are the amount to be paid by the *Contractor* to the *Employer* if the *Contractor* fails to complete the *works* by the Completion Date. Under the law of England and Wales, the amount of *delay damages* should not exceed a genuine pre-estimate of the damage that would be suffered by the *Employer* as a result of the delay to Completion. The *Employer* should keep a record of the calculation of the pre-estimate.

50.6   The purpose of retention is to provide security for the *Employer* should Defects not be corrected, and additional motivation for the *Contractor* to complete the *works*.

50.7   This clause motivates the *Contractor* to submit a first programme as required by the Works Information (see notes on Works Information part 5 under 'Stage A: How an *Employer* invites tenders for a job').

Payment 51

51.1   The latest date for payment is related to the *assessment day* after the *Employer* receives the *Contractor*'s application.

51.2   For simplicity, a fixed rate of interest of 0.5% per week is stated for the calculation of interest due on late payments, with an option for the *Employer* to state a different rate in the Contract Data.

> Enter an interest rate only if a rate less than 0.5% per week of delay has been agreed.

6 Compensation events

Compensation events **60** As in other NEC contracts, compensation events are those events stated in the contract to be compensation events. If an event is not so stated, it is not a compensation event and is at the *Contractor*'s risk. If a compensation event occurs and does not arise from the *Contractor*'s fault (subclause 61.2), the *Contractor* may be compensated for any effect the event has on cost or Completion Date.

60.1 The events which are compensation events in the ECSC are stated in this clause. Any additional compensation events required for a particular contract should be stated in an additional condition of contract in the Contract Data.

60.1(1) This clause embodies the principle that a tender can only be based on the information the tenderer has when the tender is prepared.

The exception is the case when the *Employer* is willing to accept a Defect and has agreed to change the Works Information to accommodate it.

60.1(2) This relates to the *Employer*'s obligation in subclause 15.1 to allow access to and use of the *site*.

60.1(3) This relates to the *Employer*'s obligation in subclause 15.2 to provide services and things.

60.1(4) This relates to the *Employer*'s authority in subclause 30.4 to stop or not to start work.

60.1(5) This relates to any requirements for work by the *Employer*, which will usually be stated in Section 4 of the Works Information.

60.1(6) This relates to the *Employer*'s obligation in subclause 13.2 to reply to a communication within stated periods.

60.1(7) The *Employer* is able to change a decision made under the contract.

60.1(8) This relates to the *Employer*'s authority in subclause 40.1 to instruct a search for a Defect.

60.1(9) & 60.2 The criteria for judging whether physical conditions encountered within the *site* comprise a compensation event are stated in subclause 60.1(9) and expanded in subclause 60.2. The *Employer* is motivated to provide in the Site Information (see notes on Site Information under 'Stage A: How an *Employer* invites tenders for a job' and subclause 11.2(12)) all the information about the *site* and its surroundings that the *Employer* possesses, including references to relevant, publicly available information, so that it can all be taken into account by the *Contractor* in the normal course of work without a compensation event arising.

60.1(10) The *Contractor* carries the risk of adverse weather delaying work on the *site* up to a 'ceiling' defined here. The 'ceiling' can be defined at the start of a contract by a simple calculation although it will change if the Completion Date is changed. If and when the 'ceiling' is reached, each stoppage due to adverse weather that is at least a full working day may be a compensation event.

This simple approach is chosen as being appropriate for the intended uses of the ECSC without losing a clear definition of when a compensation event is triggered. It avoids the need to measure weather and compare it with statistical data on a monthly basis, as is required in the ECC.

60.1(11) This relates to the procedure stated in subclause 61.4 (see notes on subclause 61.4).

60.1(12) This relates to 'force majeure' types of circumstance. It provides potential entitlement to compensation for the effects of the event on both cost and time. In certain circumstances the event may lead to termination by the *Employer* – see subclause 90.5.

60.1(13) The difference in quantities referred to in subclause 60.1(13) is assessed in accordance with subclause 63.1.

60.1(14) This relates to the *Contractor*'s obligation to replace and repair under subclause 43.1. For example if the *Contractor* is storing materials on *site*, the *Contractor* would be expected to take steps to prevent them from being stolen, but the *Contractor* would not be expected to take precautions against the possibility of an earthquake destroying them.

Additional compensation events

Any compensation events other than those identified in subclause 60.1 that are required for a specific contract should be stated in an additional condition of contract in the Contract Data. For example, if there is a significant risk of an increase in the cost of labour due to changes in the law, the occurrence of such a change could be made a compensation event (see example of an additional condition of contract included in example A2). Any risk which it is prudent for the *Employer* to carry can be dealt with in this way.

Notifying compensation events **61**

61.1 Either the *Employer* or the *Contractor* can notify a compensation event to the other; this clause limits when the *Contractor* can do so. The *Employer* would normally instruct the *Contractor* to submit a quotation at the same time as notifying a compensation event to the *Contractor*.

The stated time limit is intended to expedite the procedure so that dealing with compensation events a long time after they have occurred is avoided. The wording of this clause has been amended because in the first edition of the ECSC the two week period was too short to be realistic in some cases and as stated it did not prevent later notification of compensation events.

61.2 This clause states the actions to be taken by the *Employer* within one week of a compensation event being notified by the *Contractor*. If the *Employer* decides that one of the four stated criteria applies, the compensation event procedure does not continue. The *Contractor* may then decide to refer the decision to the *Adjudicator* (see notes on clauses 90 and 91).

61.3 This relates to the early warning subclause 16.1 and to subclause 63.5 (see notes on subclause 63.5).

61.4 This clause provides for assessing a compensation event the effect of which is too uncertain for reasonable forecasting. For example, unforeseen concrete foundations are encountered which impede the construction of new work. The extent of the foundations is unknown. The procedure requires the *Employer* to state assumptions about the extent of the foundations on which the *Contractor* would base a quotation. If the *Employer*'s assumptions later prove to be wrong, the *Employer* notifies a correction which would trigger another compensation event under subclause 60.1(11).

Quotations for compensation events **62**

62.1 This clause describes what a quotation for a compensation event is to comprise and states the periods within which the *Contractor* is required to submit it.

62.2 If the *Employer* is considering an action which would be a compensation event (such as a possible change to the *work*), the *Employer* is able to instruct the *Contractor* to submit a quotation for the proposed event without instructing the action. The *Employer* can decide whether or not to proceed with the action on receipt of the quotation (see subclause 62.3).

62.3	This clause states the alternative replies open to the *Employer* and the time within which they are to be given.
	If the *Employer* accepts a quotation, the Prices and the Completion Date are changed in accordance with it and the contract proceeds on that new basis having taken account of the compensation event.
62.4	This clause states a procedure to follow if the *Employer* does not agree with a quotation, culminating in the *Employer* notifying the *Employer*'s own assessment. Either Party may then refer the matter to the *Adjudicator* (see notes on clause 90). In the meantime, the *Contractor* is obliged to carry out the *Employer*'s instruction (subclause 14.1).
62.5	The *Employer* can instruct the *Contractor* to submit alternative quotations for different ways of dealing with a compensation event so that the *Employer* is able to choose the option best suited to the *Employer*'s interests.
	The *Employer* is required to discuss possible ways of dealing with the event with the *Contractor* before instructing him to submit quotations. This is intended to avoid wasting the *Contractor*'s resources in preparing quotations for methods which are not practicable.

Assessing compensation events

63	Clause 63 states how the effects of compensation events on the Prices and the Completion Date are assessed. This is the same whether the assessment is done by the *Contractor*, the *Employer* or the *Adjudicator*. The methods of assessing the changes to the Prices or rates are dealt with in subclauses 63.1, 63.2 and 63.3 and of assessing a delay to the Completion Date in subclause 63.4.
63.1	This subclause describes the assessment procedure used when the compensation event only affects the quantities of work to be done under items in the Price List for which a quantity and rate are stated. For simplicity, the rates in the Price List are used to price the changed quantities.
63.2	This subclause states the procedure used for all other compensation events and should be read in conjunction with subclause 63.3 and the definition of Defined Cost in subclause 11.2(5).
	The effect of the compensation event on the Defined Cost is assessed either as recorded for work already done or as forecast for work yet to be done (see notes on subclause 11.2(5)).
	The percentages for overheads and profit quoted in the *Contractor*'s Offer (see notes on 'Stage B: How a tenderer makes an offer' and example B1) are applied to any change in the Defined Cost due to the compensation event. Each percentage is required to cover all costs and overheads not included in the Defined Cost as well as an allowance for profit. One percentage is applied to all Defined Cost except people. A separate percentage is used for people because this may be at a different level.
63.3	'Defined Cost' is defined in subclause 11.2(5). This clause states how Defined Cost is qualified and establishes the deductions made from it in the assessment of the effects of compensation events.
63.4	If the *Contractor*'s planned Completion is delayed by the forecast effect of a compensation event, the Completion Date is delayed by the same period.
63.5	This relates to subclause 61.3 and is intended to encourage the *Contractor* to give early warnings.
63.6	Allowances for risk are to be included in forecasts of Defined Cost and Completion in the same way that the *Contractor* allows for them when pricing the tender.
63.7	This clause is intended to protect the *Employer* against inefficiency on the part of the *Contractor*.
63.8	The Party who provides the Works Information carries the risk of any ambiguities or inconsistencies in it.

63.9   This clause emphasises the finality of the assessment of compensation events. If the forecast of the effect on Defined Cost or delay included in the accepted or notified assessment proves to be wrong when the work is done, the assessment is not changed. The only circumstances in which a review is possible (by means of a further compensation event) are those stated in subclause 61.4.

7 Title

Objects and materials **70**
within the *site* 70.1   The *Contractor* should ask for an instruction from the *Employer* if something 'of value or of historical or other interest' is found. Such an instruction may be a compensation event (e.g. subclause 60.1(1)).

70.2   The Works Information should state which materials from excavation and demolition are to be the property of the *Contractor* and any conditions regarding their removal from the Site. Note that this clause reverses the 'traditional' approach, which is that the *Contractor* owns the materials that arise from demolition and site clearance.

8 Indemnity, insurance and liability

The method of dealing with the *Employer*'s and *Contractor*'s risks used in the ECSC is different to the approach included in the ECC.

The *Contractor*'s liability to Provide the Works is stated in the ECSC in subclauses such as 20.1 and 41.1. Certain financial risks, however, constitute compensation events in subclause 60.1. Additional conditions of contract stated in the Contract Data may include further compensation events.

Limitation of liability **80**
80.1   This clause deals with the aspects of liability which concern contractors most.

The first sentence concerns the *Contractor*'s liability for loss of and damage to the *Employer*'s property. This would normally be unlimited unless a limit is set as required by this clause (see example A2). The amount stated in the Contract Data is generally set at not more than the cover provided by the insurance required in terms of the contract. In effect, the *Contractor* is then only exposed to the amount of the deductible for any one claim.

This subclause limits the *Contractor*'s exposure to what are commonly referred to as consequential or indirect losses incurred by the *Employer*.

Insurance cover **82**
82.1   The *Contractor*'s responsibility for providing insurances is stated in this clause, which includes the Insurance Table. The duration of insurance cover is stated in the third column of the Insurance Table. The *Employer* is required to state in the Contract Data the extent of the insurances the *Employer* is providing (if any) and the minimum amount of cover for the third and fourth insurances in the Insurance Table.

9 Termination and dispute resolution

Termination and reasons for termination	**90** 90.1	The *Employer* is obliged to issue a termination certificate if either Party wishes to terminate in accordance with subclauses 90.2, 90.3, 90.4 or 90.5. The *Contractor* then does no further work.
	90.2, 90.3, 90.4 & 90.5	The *Employer* may terminate for any reason. The *Contractor* may terminate only for the particular reasons stated.
Procedures on termination	**91** 91.1	The *Employer* will secure title to any Plant and Materials on the *site* when the *Employer* has paid for them. This will be achieved by the payment on termination (see subclause 92.1). The *Contractor* is only required to remove Equipment.
Payment on termination	**92** 92.1	This subclause lists the components that are always included in the amount due on termination.
	92.2 & 92.3	These subclauses state further components which are included in the amount due when termination has occurred for particular reasons. They reflect the different reasons for termination.
		Reason 8 is deliberately not mentioned in these subclauses. If Reason 8 is the cause of termination the amount due is only that stated in subclause 92.1.
Dispute resolution	**93**	The simple adjudication procedure provided is designed to be appropriate for the type of work likely to be undertaken under the ECSC. In contracts where the UK Housing Grants, Construction and Regeneration Act 1996 applies, subclause 94.1 replaces subclause 93.3(1), to make the procedure comply with the Act.
	93.1	This subclause establishes the principle, followed in other NEC contracts, that any dispute which cannot be resolved by the Parties themselves must be decided by the *Adjudicator* who is independent of the Parties and is required to act impartially.
The *Adjudicator*	93.2(1)	The person appointed as *Adjudicator* should normally be named in the Contract Data. The *Adjudicator*'s impartiality and independence must be ensured. It is recommended that possible names are suggested by the *Employer* in the invitation to tender so that the *Contractor* can agree a name for inclusion in the final Contract Data (see examples A2 and C3). Acceptance of the *Contractor*'s Offer signifies agreement to the named *Adjudicator*.

The *Adjudicator* should be a person with practical experience of the kind of work to be provided by the *Contractor*. The *Adjudicator* should be able to

- understand the procedures embodied in the ECSC,
- understand the roles of both the *Employer* and the *Contractor* in the ECSC,
- act impartially and in a spirit of independence of the Parties,
- understand and have access to costs at current market rates,
- understand and have access to information on planning times and productivities,
- appreciate risks and how allowances for them should be set and
- obtain other specialist advice when required.

Under the NEC Adjudicator's Contract the *Adjudicator* is appointed jointly by the Parties. Unless the Parties agree otherwise, his charges (fees and expenses) are shared equally between the Parties, regardless of the *Adjudicator*'s decision on the dispute.

93.2(2) This subclause makes provision for the appointment of an *Adjudicator* when necessary. This will be because one was not identified in the Contract Data, or the originally chosen *Adjudicator* is no longer able to act. Initially, the Parties should try to reach agreement on a suitable person. If they cannot agree, the *Adjudicator nominating body* named in the Contract Data will make the choice for them. In the UK the Construction Industry Council and the professional institutions have lists of adjudicators from which the *Adjudicator* may be selected.

The adjudication 93.3(1) In order to ensure the early declaration of a dispute and expedite its resolution, time limits are stated. After notification of a dispute a minimum of two weeks (maximum four weeks) has to elapse before the dispute can be referred to the *Adjudicator*. This is intended to allow and encourage the Parties to resolve the dispute themselves. Compliance with the time periods stated in this clause is crucially important otherwise the dispute is barred from referral to the *Adjudicator*.

93.3(2) & (3) These subclauses set time limits for providing information to the *Adjudicator*, and allow the *Adjudicator* to issue any instructions necessary to help him in reaching a decision.

93.3(5) This requires the *Adjudicator* to use the procedures for assessing compensation events in clause 63 if he has to assess additional cost or delay caused to the *Contractor*.

93.3(6) The time for the *Adjudicator*'s decision is fixed, but it can be extended if necessary by agreement. If the decision is not given within the time required, and no further time is agreed, a Party can act as though the *Adjudicator* had resigned. This allows the Party to have a replacement *Adjudicator* appointed under subclause 93.2(2).

Review by the *tribunal* 93.4 Under subclause 93.3(8) the *Adjudicator*'s decision is binding unless and until it is revised by the *tribunal*. A dispute cannot be referred to the *tribunal* unless it has first been referred to the *Adjudicator*.

This subclause states the circumstances in which a referral can be made with a time limit for notifying a Party's intention to do so. The *Employer* identifies the *tribunal* in the Contract Data (see example A2). The choice will normally be between arbitration and the courts, either being competent to give a legally final and binding decision on the dispute. It is important to be aware of the different choices that are available when making the decision about the *tribunal*. Different laws and arbitration procedures exist in different countries, whilst in some countries no arbitration exists at all. If the *tribunal* is arbitration, the arbitration procedure to be used is also stated in the Contract Data (see example A2).

94.1 If the United Kingdom Housing Grants, Construction and Regeneration Act 1996 (referred to as 'the Act' in the following notes) applies to the contract, subclause 93.3(1) is replaced by this subclause. It is not necessary to select the changed clause in the Contract Data; the drafting of the clause means that the substitution will be automatic if the Act applies.

The provisions of subclause 93.3(1) do not comply with the Act although the principle of independent adjudication of disputes has been a key feature of the NEC family since its first publication in 1991. An objective in all NEC contracts is to overcome, where possible, the causes of disputes and, where they still arise, to motivate their clear definition and early resolution.

Subclause 94.1 allows for adjudication 'at any time'. Whilst this does not provide the early certainty that subclause 93.3(1) provides, it has been included to enable the procedure to comply with the Act so that the 'Scheme for Construction Contracts' does not apply.

JOINING SUBCONTRACT DISPUTES WITH MAIN CONTRACT DISPUTES

The following notes apply whether subclause 93.3(1) or subclause 94.1 is used.

Under subclause 21.1, the *Contractor* is responsible for all subcontractors. It is recommended that the *Adjudicator* named in the main contract is also appointed to act in all subcontracts, subject, of course, to the agreement of the subcontractor concerned.

If the *Contractor* wishes to have any matter arising under or in connection with a subcontract that impinges on a main contract matter decided with the main contract matter, the following clause should be included in the main contract.

Combining procedures 93.5

If there is a matter arising under or in connection with a subcontract to this contract which is also a matter arising under or in connection with this contract

- the *Contractor* notifies the subcontractor that the subcontractor may attend the meeting between the Parties or
- the *Contractor* may submit the subcontract matter to the *Adjudicator* at the same time as the main contract matter.

Decisions are made on the two matters together and references to the Parties include the subcontractor.

SUPPLEMENTARY GUIDANCE NOTES FOR THE ECSS

The NEC3 Engineering and Construction Short Subcontract (ECSS) can be used as a subcontract to NEC3 Engineering and Construction Contract (ECC) and NEC3 Engineering and Construction Short Contract (ECSC). It should be used with subcontracts which do not require sophisticated management techniques, comprise straightforward work and impose only low risks on both the *Contractor* and the *Subcontractor*.

For this section of the guidance notes the word *Subcontractor* is printed in italics if it is used in reference to the ECSS. The ECSS is based on the ECSC in order to achieve identical working for similar contract situations. The reason for this is that the relationship between the *Contractor* and the *Subcontractor* under ECSS is similar to that between the *Employer* and *Contractor* under ECSC. There are, however, certain additions and amendments required in the subcontract which arise from the main contract.

The ECC includes (amongst others) the following parties

- the *Employer*
- the *Project Manager*, and
- the *Supervisor*.

The ECSC includes (amongst others) the following parties

- the *Employer* and
- the *Contractor*.

The parties in the ECSS are the *Contractor* and the *Subcontractor,* but there is provision in the subcontract for naming the main contract *Employer*, *Project Manager*, *Supervisor* and Adjudicator.

The ECSC pricing mechanism in the Price List has been retained for the subcontract. Thus, for example, the main contract may be a lump sum contract and the subcontract may be a lump sum or a remeasurement contract or a combination of the two.

To avoid confusion with the ECSC, the following item has been prefixed 'subcontract'

- *works*.

Other changes from ECSC are

- Subsubcontractor for Subcontractor, and
- Subcontract Data for Contract Data,

The following items retain the same terms as in the ECSC but will have different provisions accordingly

- *starting date*,
- Completion Date, and
- Works Information.

The main additions and amendments arising from provisions of the main contract are described below.

Subcontract documents

Provision for the required information about the main contract has been included in the ECSS and the boxed guidance notes have been extended where appropriate.

In preparing the subcontract the *Contractor* must be precise in detailing the documentation which comprises both the Works Information and the Site Information for the ECSS. It is not sufficient for the *Contractor* to merely generalise by, for example, stating 'The main contract Works Information and Site Information shall be incorporated into this subcontract'. A properly drafted

subcontract must state what these documents are; this will be particularly important if the *Contractor* decides upon a pricing mechanism for the subcontract different to that under the main contract.

The *Contractor* may choose a pricing mechanism for the subcontract consistent with that of the main contract. However, the best pricing mechanism should be chosen for each subcontract and therefore the *Contractor* may engage a subcontractor under a different pricing mechanism: for example, where the *Subcontractor* is offering a lump sum price but the *Contractor* is under a remeasurement contract.

It is usual for the subcontract Works Information to be based upon and comprise documentation such as specification and drawings. Similarly, subcontract Site Information will most probably be that from the main contract but might be added to by the *Contractor* if, for example, he has carried out further site investigation work prior to seeking to sublet a part of the *works*.

Hence where the *Contractor* is incorporating main contract data into a subcontract, precise schedules should be prepared and expressly identified in the Subcontract Data part one.

It may be desirable for the *Subcontractor* to have knowledge of the full general main contract documentation. In this case the *Subcontractor* should be given a copy or, as is more usual, he is given access to the documents to inspect them and extract copies of any relevant parts. Either way it is recommended that the relevant parts of the main contract documentation are incorporated in the subcontract by reference in the Subcontract Data.

Because of the inevitable difference in obligations between the main contract and subcontract there are some special considerations which the parties to the subcontract should be aware of.

Disputes

A provision has been included to cater for a dispute arising under the main contract which concerns the subcontract works. This enables the *Contractor* to require that such a dispute can be dealt with jointly with the dispute under the main contract by the main contract Adjudicator. This avoids two different adjudicators making different decisions on the same dispute.

The subcontract *Adjudicator* may be a person different from the main contract Adjudicator. His function is to deal with disputes which arise only between the *Contractor* and *Subcontractor* and which do not concern the *Employer*.

If any of the three parties to a joint dispute disagrees with the Adjudicator's decision, he may refer it to the *tribunal*, as in the case of a dispute between only two contracting parties.

Termination

If the main contract is terminated, the *Contractor* will wish to terminate the subcontracts. The payment consequences depend upon whether the termination is due to the *Subcontractor*'s default or not.

Time periods

Time periods stated in the ECSS have been adjusted to allow for associated actions under the main contract. Time limits in the subcontract for sending information to the *Contractor* are less than the times stated in the main contract for sending information to the *Employer* in order to allow time for the *Contractor* to incorporate or process the information. Time limits in the subcontract for transmitting decisions or payments to the *Subcontractor* are greater than the equivalent times stated in the main contract, for similar reasons.

Some time periods are not stated in the ECSS but, like the main contract, are to be inserted in the Subcontract Data. An example is a reply to a communication.

The *Contractor* must ensure that the time periods in the Subcontract Data are adequate for proper reply but not excessive so as to prevent the *Contractor* from sending a similar reply under the main contract.

Insurance

The insurances stated in the Insurance Table follow those in the equivalent in the ECSC, except certain provisions being in respect of the *subcontract works* (in ECSS) rather than the *works* (in ECSC). Double insurance is largely avoided since the insurance premiums payable by the *Contractor* under the main contract will reflect the proportion of the *works* which are subcontracted.

Under the ECSS the risks carried by the *Contractor* for the *works* subcontracted are passed to the *Subcontractor* for the period from the subcontract *starting date* until the subcontract Defects Certificate has been issued. Outside of this period, with the exception of continuing liabilities, the *Contractor* or *Employer* (depending upon other main contract criteria) carries the risk for the subcontract *works*. Thus if the subcontract *completion date* and *defects date* are earlier than those of the main contract then the *Contractor* must recognise two important factors.

- The *Contractor* will carry the risk of and should ensure that his insurance cover is continuing for the *subcontract works*.
- The *Contractor* will carry the risk of Defects in the *subcontract works* from the conclusion of the *Subcontractor*'s liability for correcting his Defects upon the issue of the subcontract Defects Certificate.

Should it be important, for example, that the *Subcontractor* continues to correct Defects right up to Completion of the whole of the works in the main contract (or even to the issue of the main contract Defects Certificate) then the Subcontract Data part one must properly reflect and include this intention of the Parties by incorporating the completion date of the whole of the works in the main contract and an appropriate subcontract *defects date* after completion of the whole of the works in the main contract.

Notwithstanding the subcontract insurance provisions, the *Contractor* still carries responsibility for the performance of the *Subcontractor* in the ECSC and the *Subcontractor* is always responsible for insuring his own Equipment and his employees.

Delay damages

When considering *delay damages* it is not sufficient for the *Contractor* to insert in the Subcontract Data optional statements general wording such as 'delay damages as main contract'. The damages must be a genuine pre-estimate at the time when the subcontract is made of the likely losses that the *Contractor* will suffer if there is a delay by the *Subcontractor*.

If the *subcontract works* are critical or the subcontract *completion date* is coincidental with that of the main contract then it may be that the *delay damages* under the subcontract will be as those for the main contract. In circumstances where the subcontract is not critical or concerns only minor works, the *delay damages* must reflect this on the basis of a genuine pre-estimate of the loss the *Contractor* would suffer.

Guidance notes

Detailed guidance notes for the ECSS have not been prepared since the principles can be understood from the ECSC guidance notes.

Flow charts

Flow charts for the subcontract have not been prepared since the logic of the procedures can be understood from the ECSC flow charts.

Stage A   How an *Employer* invites tenders for a job

Example A1   Title page

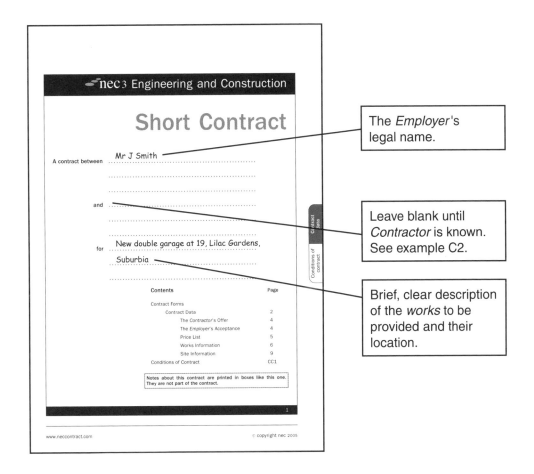

Example A2   Contract Data

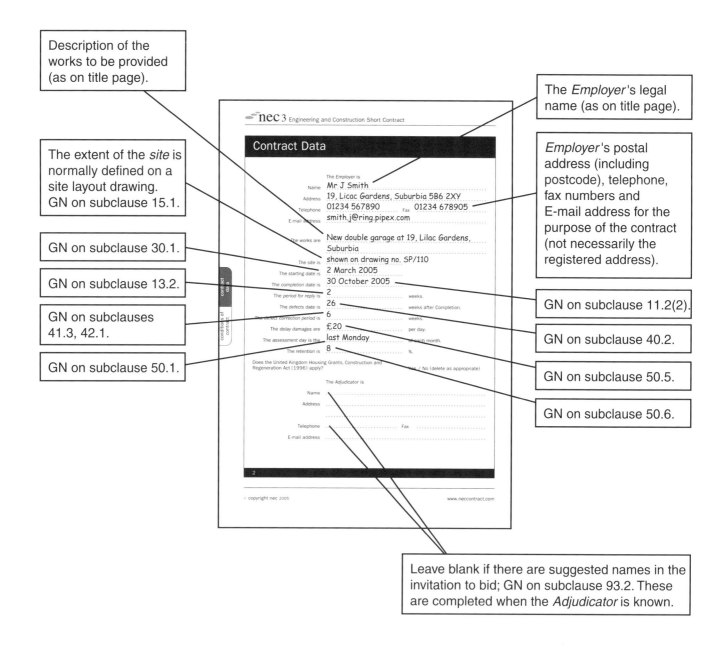

Description of the works to be provided (as on title page).

The extent of the *site* is normally defined on a site layout drawing. GN on subclause 15.1.

GN on subclause 30.1.

GN on subclause 13.2.

GN on subclauses 41.3, 42.1.

GN on subclause 50.1.

The *Employer*'s legal name (as on title page).

Employer's postal address (including postcode), telephone, fax numbers and E-mail address for the purpose of the contract (not necessarily the registered address).

GN on subclause 11.2(2).

GN on subclause 40.2.

GN on subclause 50.5.

GN on subclause 50.6.

Leave blank if there are suggested names in the invitation to bid; GN on subclause 93.2. These are completed when the *Adjudicator* is known.

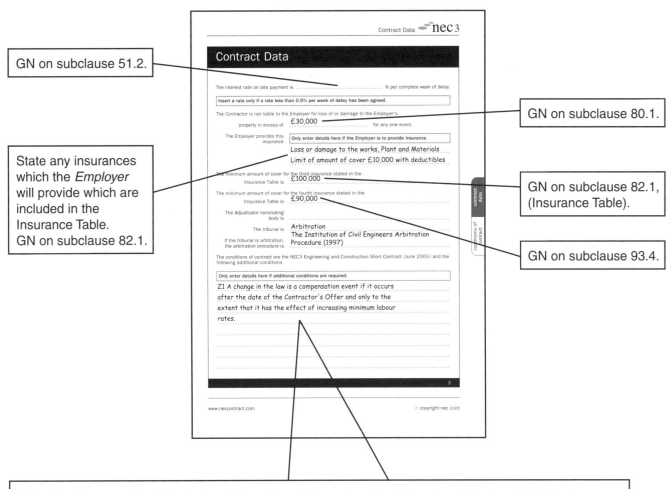

GN on subclause 51.2.

State any insurances which the *Employer* will provide which are included in the Insurance Table. GN on subclause 82.1.

GN on subclause 80.1.

GN on subclause 82.1, (Insurance Table).

GN on subclause 93.4.

If the *Employer* requires to include additional conditions of contract they should be inserted in the box provided at the end of the Contract Data. Any additional conditions should be drafted in the same style as the ECSC clauses, using the name defined terms and other terminology. They should be carefully checked, preferably by flowcharting, to ensure that they mesh with the ECSC clauses.

Additional conditions should be used only when absolutely necessary to accommodate special needs which are not covered by the ECSC clauses. Such special needs may be those peculiar to the country where the work is to be done.

See notes on additional compensation events under subclause 60.1.

Many special needs can be accommodated during the invitation to tender, by insertions in the Works Information and by appropriate use of the Price List.

Stage B   How a tenderer makes an offer

Example B1   The *Contractor*'s Offer

The tenderer's legal name.

Tenderer's postal address (including postcode), telephone and fax numbers and E-mail address for the purpose of the contract.

Offer to be signed by a person in the tenderer's organisation having the necessary authority.

Left blank until completed at a later stage by the *Employer*. See example C1.

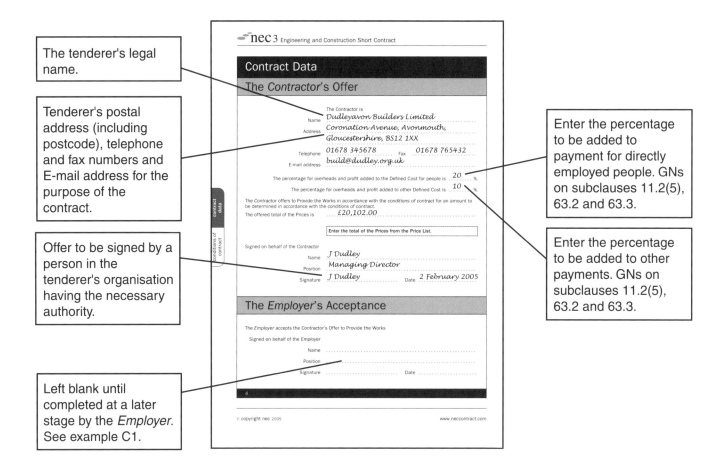

Enter the percentage to be added to payment for directly employed people. GNs on subclauses 11.2(5), 63.2 and 63.3.

Enter the percentage to be added to other payments. GNs on subclauses 11.2(5), 63.2 and 63.3.

Stage C   How a contract is made

Example C1   The *Employer*'s acceptance

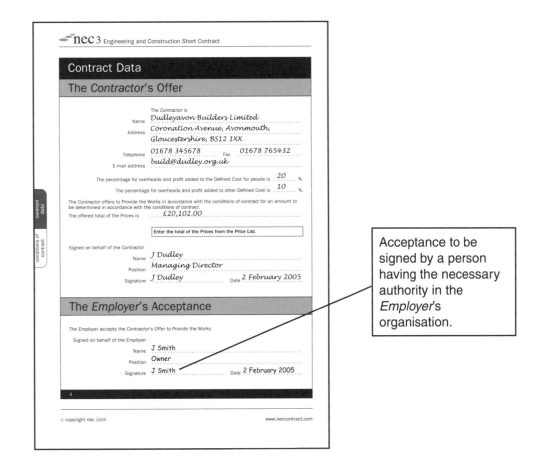

Acceptance to be signed by a person having the necessary authority in the *Employer*'s organisation.

Example C2   Title page

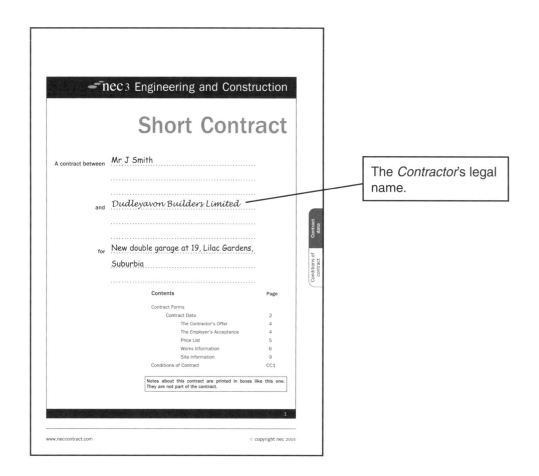

Example C3   Contract Data

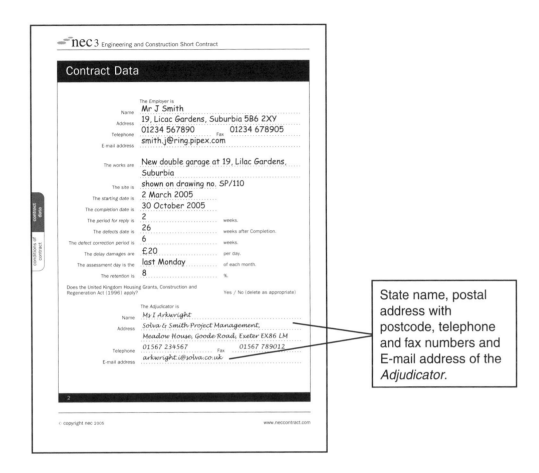

nec 3 Engineering and Construction Short Contract

Contract Data

The *Employer* is
Name   Mr J Smith
Address   19, Lilac Gardens, Suburbia 5B6 2XY
Telephone   01234 567890   Fax   01234 678905
E-mail address   smith.j@ring.pipex.com

The *works* are   New double garage at 19, Lilac Gardens, Suburbia
The *site* is   shown on drawing no. SP/110
The *starting date* is   2 March 2005
The *completion date* is 30 October 2005
The *period for reply* is 2 .... weeks.
The *defects date* is   26 .... weeks after Completion.
The *defect correction period* is 6 .... weeks.
The *delay damages* are   £20 .... per day.
The *assessment day* is the last Monday .... of each month.
The *retention* is   8 .... %.

Does the United Kingdom Housing Grants, Construction and
Regeneration Act (1996) apply?   Yes / No (delete as appropriate)

The *Adjudicator* is
Name   Mr I Arkwright
Address   Solva & Smith Project Management,
              Meadow House, Goode Road, Exeter EX86 LM
Telephone   01567 234567   Fax   01567 789012
E-mail address   arkwright.i@solva.co.uk

2

State name, postal address with postcode, telephone and fax numbers and E-mail address of the *Adjudicator*.

Normally there should be no changes to the second page of the Contract Data unless agreed by the Parties.

MULTI-PARTY PARTNERING

Introduction

A partnering contract, between two Parties only, is achieved by using a standard NEC contract. If partnering is required between two or more parties working on the same project or programme of projects, then amendments are required to the ECSC. In other NEC contracts, secondary Option X12 Partnering is provided to achieve this arrangement. The ECSC does not have a secondary Options structure so a stand alone clause has been drafted using X12 as a basis. This stand alone clause is referred to as the ECSC multi-party partnering clause in this document. This clause can be used alongside other contracts using X12. Similar amendments would be necessary if the multi-party arrangement was to be extended to a subcontractor appointed using the ECSS.

The parties who have the ECSC multi-party partnering clause included in their contracts are all the bodies who are intended to make up the project partnering team. The ECSC multi-party partnering clause does not create a multi-party contract.

This clause does not duplicate provisions of the appropriate existing conditions of contract in the NEC family that will be used for the individual contracts. It follows normal NEC structure in that it is made up of clauses, data and information.

The content is derived from the Guide to Project Team Partnering published by the Construction Industry Council (CIC). The requirements of the CIC document that are not already in the NEC bi-party contract is covered in this clause. The structure of the NEC family of contracts means the ECSC multi-party partnering clause will not work unless an NEC contract is used.

The purpose of this clause (and Option X12 Partnering) is to establish the NEC family as an effective contract basis for multi-party partnering. As with all NEC documents it is intended that the range of application should be wide. By linking this clause (or X12) to appropriate bi-party contracts, it is intended that the NEC can be used

- for partnering for any number of projects (i.e. single project or multi-project),
- internationally,
- for projects of any technical composition, and
- as far down the supply chain as required.

This clause is given legal effect by including it in the appropriate bi-party contract. It is not a free standing contract but a part of each bi-party contract that is common to all contracts in a project team.

The underlying bi-party contract will be for a contribution of any type, the work content or objective which is sufficiently defined to permit a conventional NEC contract to be signed.

Parties must recognise that by entering into a contract with the ECSC multi-party partnering clause they will be undertaking responsibilities additional to those in the basic NEC contract.

A dispute (or difference) between Partners who do not have a contract between themselves is resolved by the Core Group. This is the Group that manages the conduct of the Partners in accordance with the Partnering Information. If the Core Group is unable to resolve the issue, then it is resolved under the procedure of the Partners' Own Contracts, either directly or indirectly with the *Client*, who will always be involved at some stage in the contractual chain. The *Client* may seek to have the issues on all contracts dealt with simultaneously.

The ECSC multi-party partnering clause does not include direct remedies between non-contracting Partners to recover losses suffered by one of them caused by a failure of the other. These remedies remain available in each Partner's Own Contract, but their existence will encourage the parties to compromise any differences that arise.

This applies at all levels of the supply chain, as a *Contractor* who is a Partner retains the responsibility for actions of a subcontractor who is a Partner.

The final sanction against any Partner who fails to act as stated in the ECSC multi-party partnering clause is for the Partner who employed them not to invite them to partner again.

Additional Contract Data for the ECSC multi-party partnering clause

The *Client* is the Party for whom the projects are being carried out. He may also be the *Employer* in an NEC contract.

The *Client*'s objective is the objective for the 'programme of projects' if more than one or for 'the project' if only one. The objective should be expressed quantitatively if possible (the business case). It should also include the partnering objectives.

Partnering Information includes any requirements for

- use of common information systems, sharing of offices,
- attendance at Partners' and Core Group meetings,
- participation in partnering workshops,
- arrangements for joint design development,
- value engineering and value management,
- risk management, and
- other matters that the Core Group manages.

This information should not duplicate requirements in the bi-party contracts.

The additional Contract Data for the ECSC multi-party partnering clause, like other Contract Data in the NEC contracts, does not change. The Schedule of Partners and the Schedule of Core Group Members, like the Activity Schedule and other schedules referred to in the Contract Data do change from time to time. The following are samples of the typical information required in these schedules.

Schedule of Partners

Date of last revision: ....

The Partners are the following.

Name of Partner	Representative's address and contact details	Contribution and objective	Joining date	Leaving date	Key Performance Indicator	Target	Measurement arrangement	Amount of Payment if the target is improved upon or achieved*

* Enter *nil* in the last column if there is to be no money incentive

Schedule of Core Group Members

Date of last revision: ....

The Core Group members are the *Client* and the following.

Name of Partner	Address and contact details	Joining date	Leaving date

Including the ECSC multi-party partnering clause in the Own Contracts

The ECSC multi-party partnering clause is incorporated into the Own Contract of a Partner as follows.

1. The additional conditions below (referred to as Z1 but should be numbered to suit) would be inserted in the 'additional conditions' provision in the Contract Data on page 3.

2. Add the following entry to the Contract Data in each bi-party contract:

ECSC multi-party partnering

- The *Client* is

    Name...

    Address ....

    ....

    - The *Client*'s *objective* is.......................................

        ....

        ....

        ....

        ....

        ....

        ....

    - The Partnering Information is in

        ....

        ....

        ....

        ....

ECSC multi-party partnering

Z1: Partnering

Identified and defined terms Z1.1

(1) The Partners are those named in the Schedule of Partners. The *Client* is a Partner.

(2) An Own Contract is a contract between two Partners which includes this clause.

(3) The Core Group comprises the Partners listed in the Schedule of Core Group Members.

(4) Partnering Information is information which specifies how the Partners work together and is either in the documents which the Contract Data states it is in or in an instruction given in accordance with this contract.

(5) A Key Performance Indicator is an aspect of performance for which a target is stated in the Schedule of Partners.

Actions Z1.2

(1) Each Partner works with the other Partners to achieve the *Client's objective* stated in the Contract Data and the objectives of every other Partner stated in the Schedule of Partners.

(2) Each Partner nominates a representative to act for it in dealings with other Partners.

(3) The Core Group acts and takes decisions on behalf of the Partners on those matters stated in the Partnering Information.

(4) The Partners select the members of the Core Group. The Core Group decides how they will work and decides the dates when each member joins and leaves the Core Group. The *Client*'s representative leads the Core Group unless stated otherwise in the Partnering Information.

(5) The Core Group keeps the Schedule of Core Group Members and the Schedule of Partners up to date and issues copies of them to the Partners each time either is revised.

(6) This clause does not create a legal partnership between Partners who are not one of the Parties in this contract.

Working together Z1.3

(1) The Partners work together as stated in the Partnering Information and in a spirit of mutual trust and co-operation.

(2) A Partner may ask another Partner to provide information which he needs to carry out the work in his Own Contract and the other Partner provides it.

(3) Each Partner gives an early warning to the other Partners when he becomes aware of any matter that could affect the achievement of another Partner's objectives stated in the Schedule of Partners.

(4) The Partners use common information systems as set out in the Partnering Information.

(5) A Partner implements a decision of the Core Group by issuing instructions in accordance with its Own Contracts.

(6) The Core Group may give an instruction to the Partners to change the Partnering Information. Each such change to the Partnering Information is a compensation event which may lead to reduced Prices.

(7) The Core Group prepares and maintains a timetable showing the proposed timing of the contributions of the Partners. The Core Group issues a copy of the timetable to the Partners each time it is revised. The *Contractor* changes his programme if it is necessary to do so in order to comply with the revised timetable. Each such change is a compensation event which may lead to reduced Prices.

(8) A Partner gives advice, information and opinion to the Core Group and to other Partners when asked to do so by the Core Group. This advice, information and opinion relates to work that another Partner is carrying out under its Own Contract and is given fully, openly and objectively. The Partners show contingency and risk allowances in information about costs, prices and timing for future work.

(9) A Partner notifies the Core Group before subcontracting any work.

Incentives Z1.4 (1) A Partner is paid the amount stated in the Schedule of Partners if the target stated for a Key Performance Indicator is improved upon or achieved. Payment of the amount is due when the target has been improved upon or achieved and is made as part of the amount due in the Partner's Own Contract.

(2) The *Client* may add a Key Performance Indicator and associated payment to the Schedule of Partners but may not delete or reduce a payment stated in the Schedule of Partners.

Guidance notes on ECSC multi-party partnering clauses

Identified and defined terms

Clause Z1.2 (1)
The point at which someone becomes a Partner is when his Own Contract (which includes the ECSC multi-party partnering clause) comes into existence. They should then be named in the Schedule of Partners, and their representative identified.

Clause Z1.2 (3)
Not every Partner is a member of the Core Group.

Clause Z1.2 (5)
There are two options for subcontractor partners. Either the amount payable cascades down if the schedule allocates the same bonus/cost to the main contractor and subcontractor, or the main contractor absorbs the bonus/cost and does not pass it on.

Working together

Clause Z1.3 (5)
The Core Group organises and holds meetings. It produces and distributes records of each meeting which include agreed actions. Instructions from the Core Group are issued in accordance with the Partner's Own Contract. The Core Group may invite other Partners or people to a meeting of the Core Group.

Clause Z1.3 (8)
The Partners should give advice and assistance when asked, and in addition whenever they identify something that would be helpful to another Partner.

Clause Z1.3 (9)
A subcontractor/subconsultant may be a Partner, but the general policy on this should be decided at the beginning of the Project. The Core Group should advise the Contractor/Consultant at the outset if a subcontractor/subconsultant is to be asked to be a Partner. A subcontractor/subconsultant who the Core group decides should be a Partner should not be appointed if he is unwilling to be a Partner.

Incentives

Clause Z1.4 (1) (also 'Z1.1 (1) and Z1.3 (3)')
If one Partner lets the others down for a particular target by poor performance, then all lose their bonus for that target. If the *Employer* tries to prevent a target being met, he is in breach of clause 10.1.

There can be more than one KPI for each partner. KPIs may apply to one Partner, to several partners or to all partners.

An example of a KPI

KPI	Number of days to complete each floor of the building framework
Target	14 days
Measurement	Number of days between removal of falsework from the entire slab and from the slab below
Amount	Main contractor – £5,000 each floor Formwork and concrete sub-contractor – £2,000 each floor Structural designer – £750 each floor

Clause Z1.4 (2)
The *Client* should consult with the other Partners before adding a KPI. The effect on subcontracted work should be noted; adding a KPI to work which is subcontracted can involve a change to the KPI for a subcontractor/subconsultant.

Flow charts for the

Engineering and Construction Short Contract

FLOW CHARTS

PREFACE

These flow charts depict the procedures followed when using the NEC3 Engineering and Construction Short Contract (ECSC). They are intended to help people using the ECSC to see how the various ECSC clauses produce clear and precise sequences of action for the people involved.

The flow charts are not part of any contract. Much of the text and many of the words taken from the ECSC itself are abbreviated in the flow charts. The flow charts depict almost all of the sequences of action set out in the ECSC. Many of the sequences interact, and because of this, users of the flow charts will often have to review more than one sheet in order to track the full sequence of actions in one area.

PREFACE

ABBREVIATIONS USED IN THE FLOW CHART BOXES

FC 61	Flow chart for clause 61
E	*Employer*
C	*Contractor*
SC	Subcontractor
CD	Contract Data
CE	Compensation event
P&M	Plant and Materials
PWDD	Price for Work Done to Date
SI	Site Information
WI	Works Information

Legend

CHART START

HEADINGS
    Headings in caps
    provide guidance

STATEMENTS
    If a subclause is
    referenced, text
    is from the NEC

LOGIC LINKS
    Links go to right
    and/or downward
    unless shown

QUESTION
    Answer question
    to determine the
    route to follow

SUBROUTINE
    Include another
    flow chart here

CONTINUATION
    Link to matching
    point(s) on other
    chart sheets

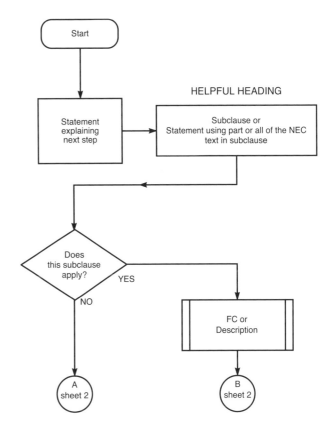

CHART TITLE
    Chart number,
    title and sheet

Flow chart or Sheet 1 of 2
Description

CONTINUATION

CHART FINISH

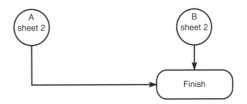

CHART TITLE

Flow chart or Sheet 2 of 2
Description

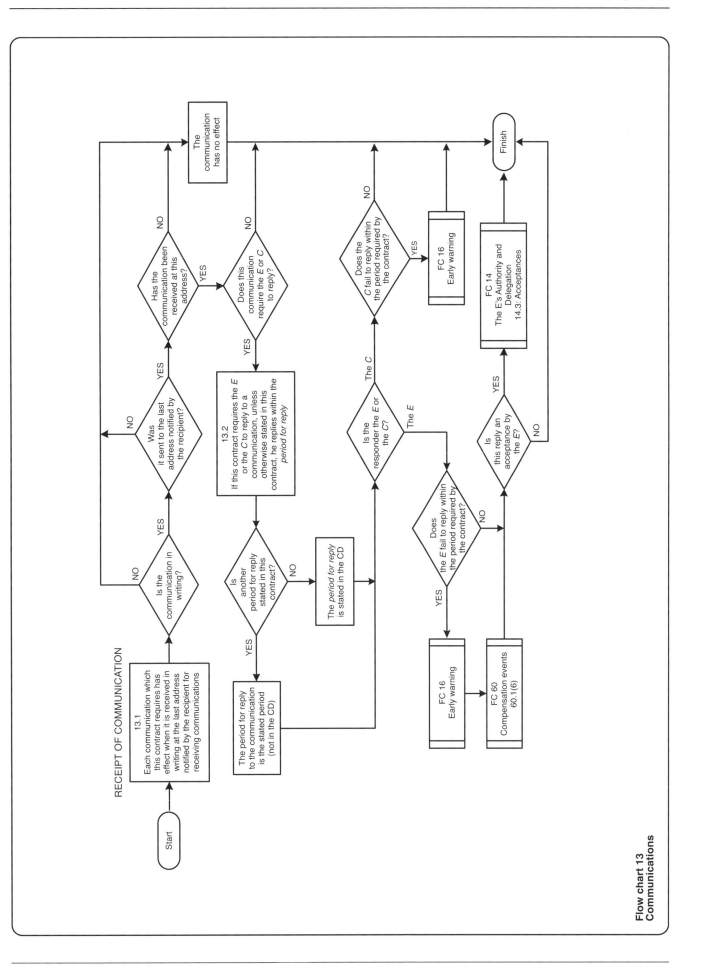

RECEIPT OF COMMUNICATION

Flow chart 13
Communications

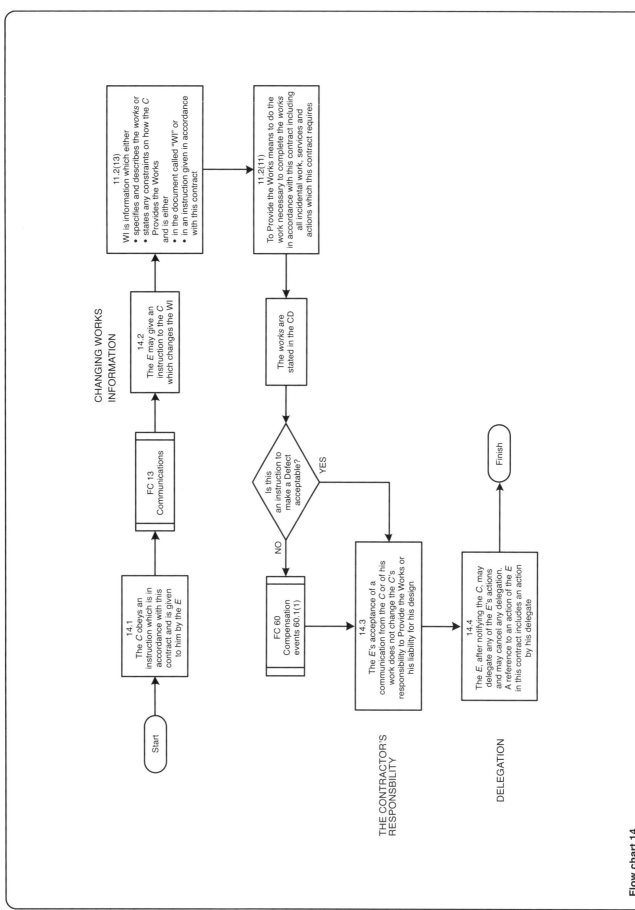

CHANGING WORKS INFORMATION

Start

14.1
The *C* obeys an instruction which is in accordance with this contract and is given to him by the *E*

FC 13
Communications

14.2
The *E* may give an instruction to the *C* which changes the WI

11.2(13)
WI is information which either
• specifies and describes the *works* or
• states any constraints on how the *C* Provides the Works
and is either
• in the document called "WI" or
• in an instruction given in accordance with this contract

11.2(11)
To Provide the Works means to do the work necessary to complete the *works* in accordance with this contract including all incidental work, services and actions which this contract requires

The *works* are stated in the CD

Is this an instruction to make a Defect acceptable?

NO / YES

FC 60
Compensation events 60.1(1)

THE CONTRACTOR'S RESPONSBILITY

14.3
The *E*'s acceptance of a communication from the *C* or of his work does not change the *C*'s responsibility to Provide the Works or his liability for his design

DELEGATION

14.4
The *E*, after notifying the *C*, may delegate any of the *E*'s actions and may cancel any delegation. A reference to an action of the *E* in this contract includes an action by his delegate

Finish

Flow chart 14
The *Employer's* authority and delegation

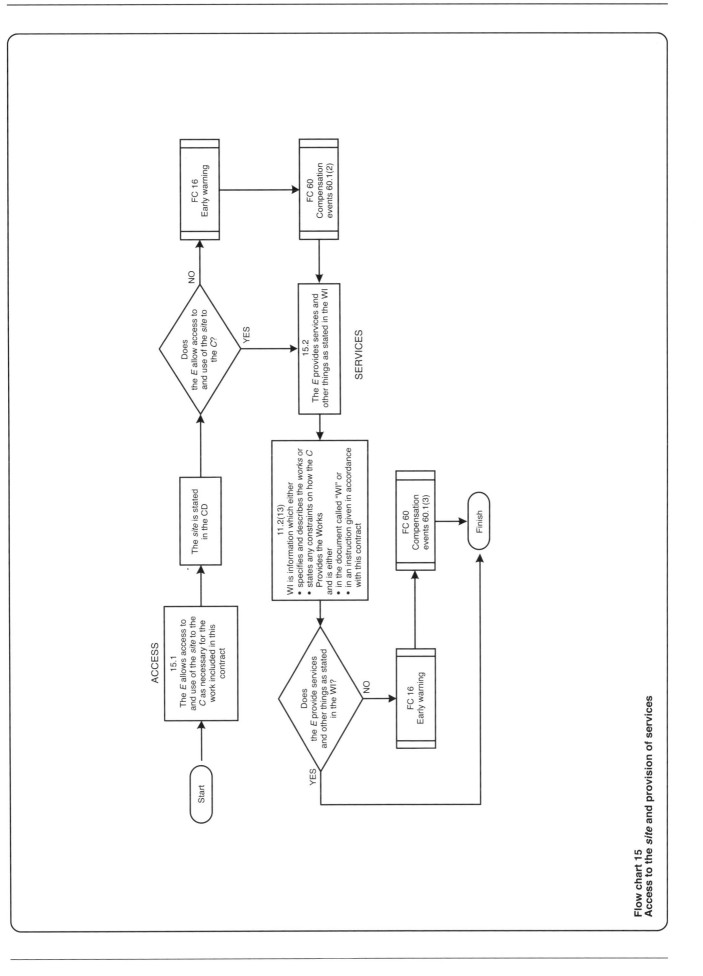

Flow chart 15
Access to the *site* and provision of services

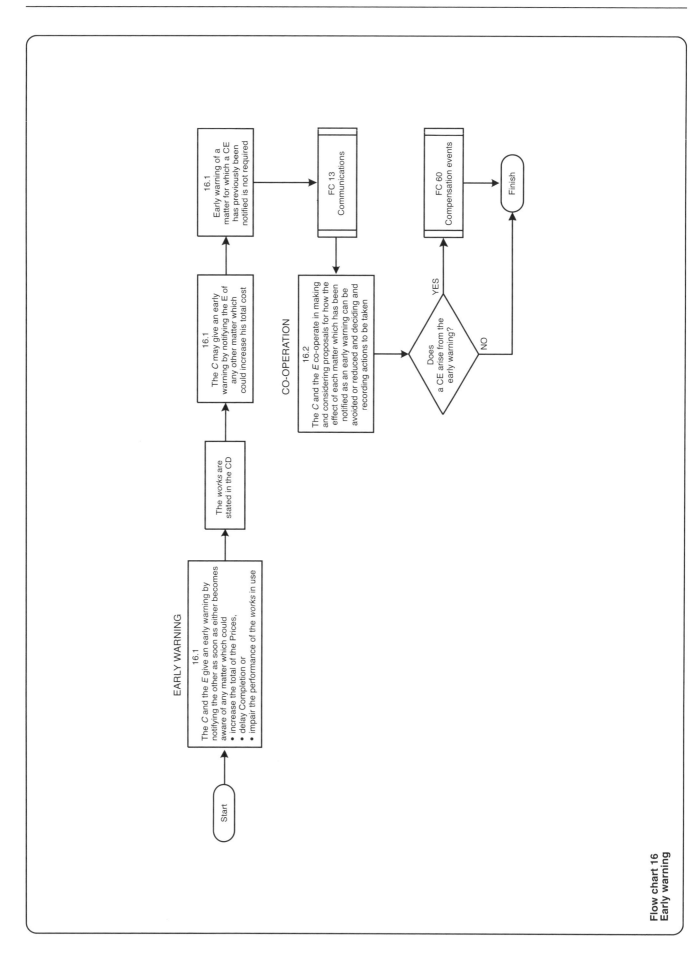

EARLY WARNING

16.1
The C and the E give an early warning by notifying the other as soon as either becomes aware of any matter which could
- increase the total of the Prices,
- delay Completion or
- impair the performance of the *works* in use

The *works* are stated in the CD

16.1
The C may give an early warning by notifying the E of any other matter which could increase his total cost

16.1
Early warning of a matter for which a CE has previously been notified is not required

FC 13
Communications

CO-OPERATION

16.2
The C and the E co-operate in making and considering proposals for how the effect of each matter which has been notified as an early warning can be avoided or reduced and deciding and recording actions to be taken

Does a CE arise from the early warning?

YES

NO

FC 60
Compensation events

Start

Finish

**Flow chart 16
Early warning**

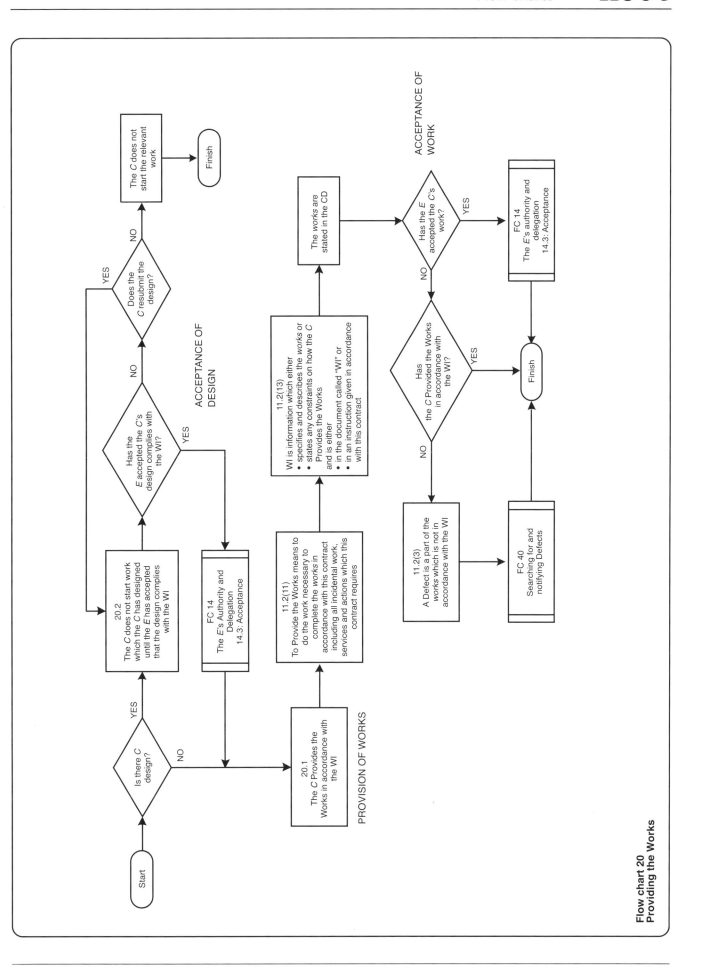

ACCEPTANCE OF
DESIGN

ACCEPTANCE OF
WORK

20.2
The C does not start work which the C has designed until the E has accepted that the design complies with the WI

FC 14
The E's Authority and Delegation
14.3: Acceptance

Has the E accepted the C's design complies with the WI?

Does the C resubmit the design?

The C does not start the relevant work

Finish

Is there C design?

20.1
The C Provides the Works in accordance with the WI

PROVISION OF WORKS

11.2(11)
To Provide the Works means to do the work necessary to complete the works in accordance with this contract including all incidental work, services and actions which this contract requires

11.2(13)
WI is information which either
• specifies and describes the works or
• states any constraints on how the C Provides the Works
and is either
• in the document called "WI" or
• in an instruction given in accordance with this contract

The works are stated in the CD

Has the E accepted the C's work?

11.2(3)
A Defect is a part of the works which is not in accordance with the WI

Has the C Provided the Works in accordance with the WI?

FC 40
Searching for and notifying Defects

Finish

FC 14
The E's authority and delegation
14.3: Acceptance

Start

Flow chart 20
Providing the Works

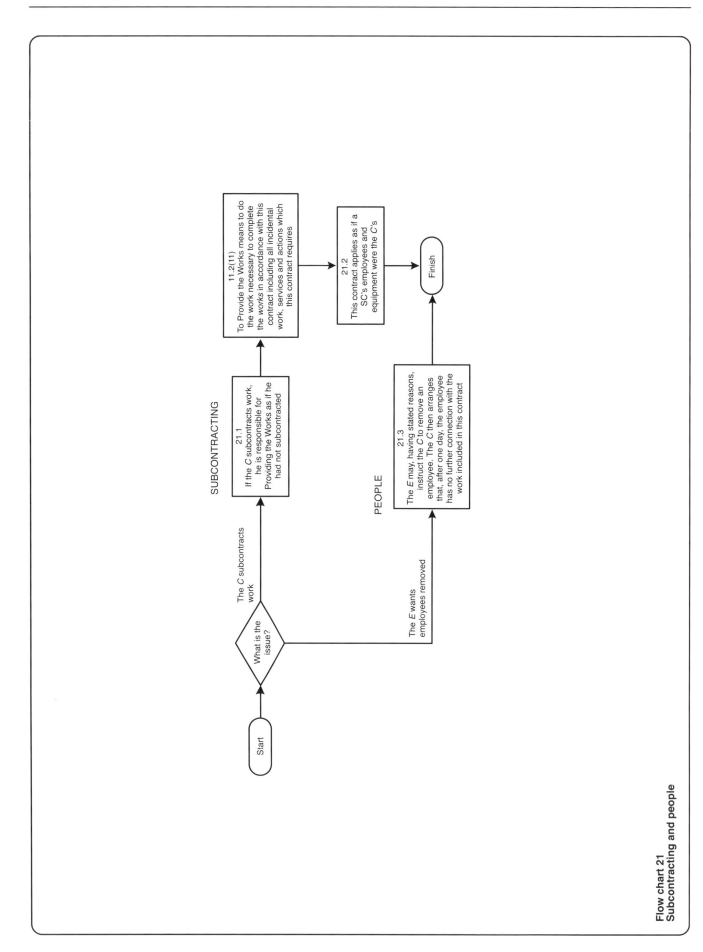

Start

What is the issue?

The C subcontracts work

SUBCONTRACTING

21.1
If the C subcontracts work, he is responsible for Providing the Works as if he had not subcontracted

11.2(11)
To Provide the Works means to do the work necessary to complete the works in accordance with this contract including all incidental work, services and actions which this contract requires

21.2
This contract applies as if a SC's employees and equipment were the C's

The E wants employees removed

PEOPLE

21.3
The E may, having stated reasons, instruct the C to remove an employee. The C then arranges that, after one day, the employee has no further connection with the work included in this contract

Finish

Flow chart 21
Subcontracting and people

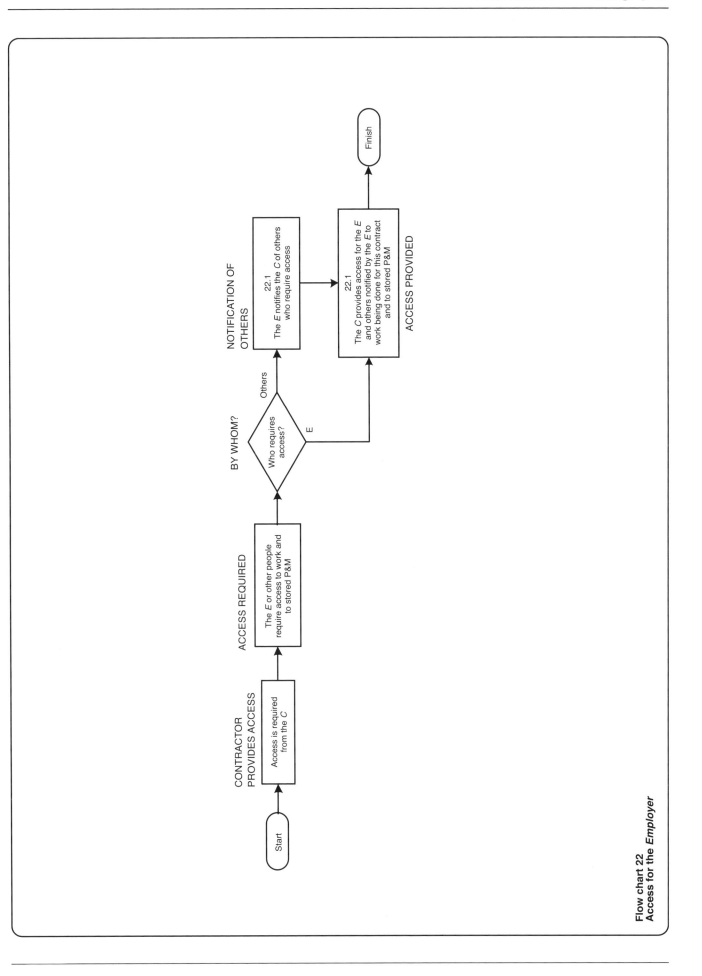

CONTRACTOR
PROVIDES ACCESS

Start

Access is required
from the *C*

ACCESS REQUIRED

The *E* or other people
require access to work and
to stored P&M

BY WHOM?

Who requires
access?

Others

E

NOTIFICATION OF
OTHERS

22.1
The *E* notifies the *C* of others
who require access

22.1
The *C* provides access for the *E*
and others notified by the *E* to
work being done for this contract
and to stored P&M

ACCESS PROVIDED

Finish

Flow chart 22
Access for the *Employer*

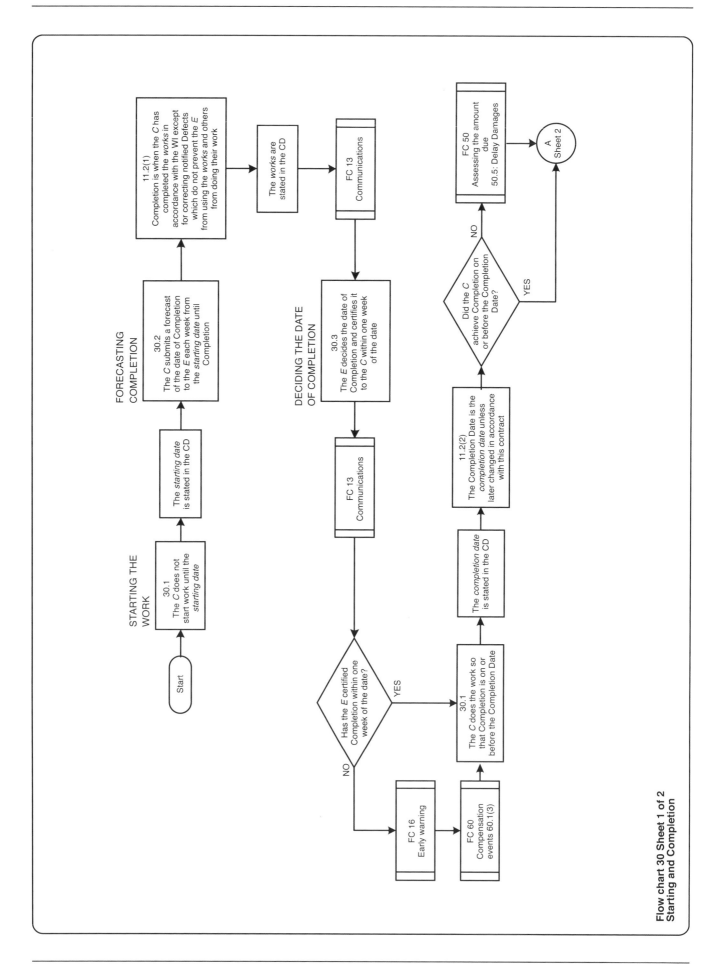

STARTING THE WORK

FORECASTING COMPLETION

DECIDING THE DATE OF COMPLETION

Start

30.1
The C does not start work until the *starting date*

The *starting date* is stated in the CD

30.2
The C submits a forecast of the date of Completion to the E each week from the *starting date* until Completion

11.2(1)
Completion is when the C has completed the *works* in accordance with the WI except for correcting notified Defects which do not prevent the E from using the *works* and others from doing their work

The *works* are stated in the CD

FC 13
Communications

30.3
The E decides the date of Completion and certifies it to the C within one week of the date

FC 13
Communications

Has the E certified Completion within one week of the date?

NO → FC 16 Early warning → FC 60 Compensation events 60.1(3)

YES → 30.1 The C does the work so that Completion is on or before the Completion Date

The *completion date* is stated in the CD

11.2(2)
The Completion Date is the *completion date* unless later changed in accordance with this contract

Did the C achieve Completion on or before the Completion Date?

NO → FC 50 Assessing the amount due 50.5: Delay Damages → A Sheet 2

YES → A Sheet 2

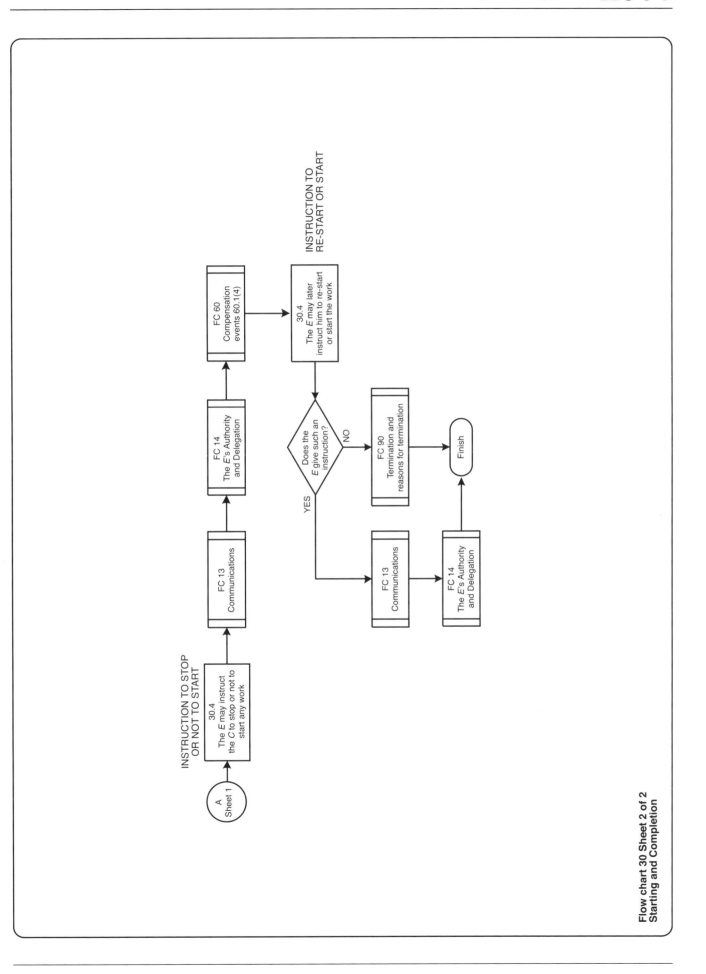

Flow chart 30 Sheet 2 of 2
Starting and Completion

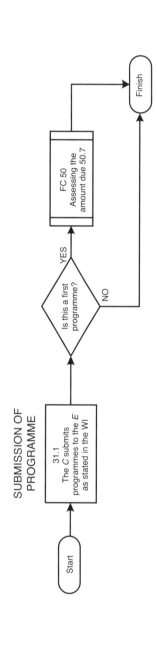

SUBMISSION OF PROGRAMME

Start

31.1
The *C* submits programmes to the *E* as stated in the WI

Is this a first programme?

YES

NO

FC 50
Assessing the amount due 50.7

Finish

Flow chart 31
The programme

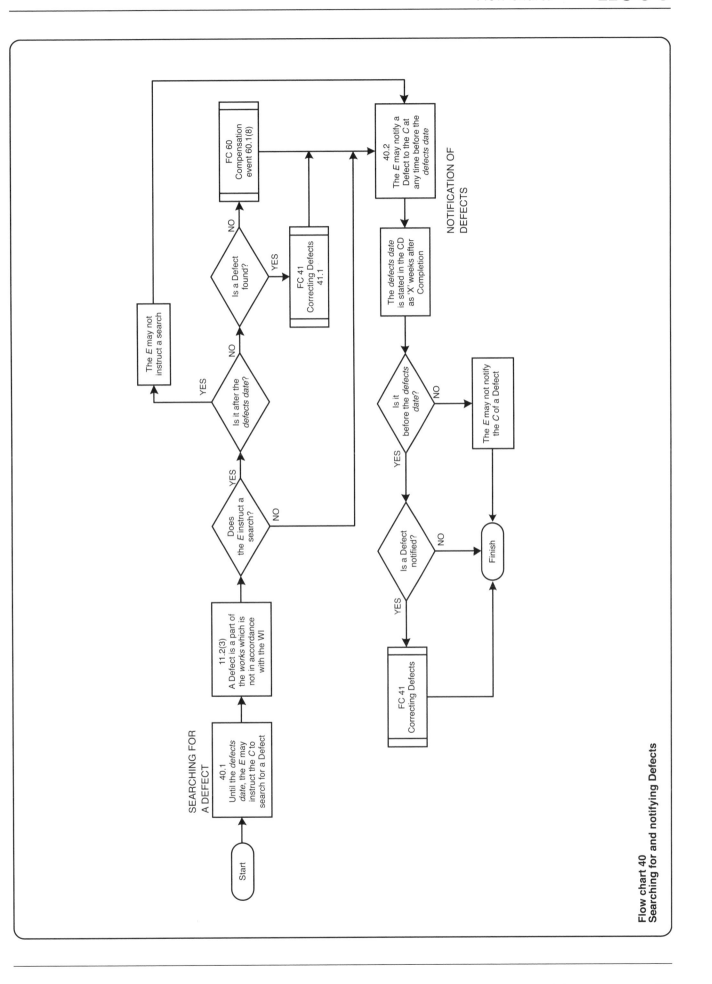

Flow chart 40
Searching for and notifying Defects

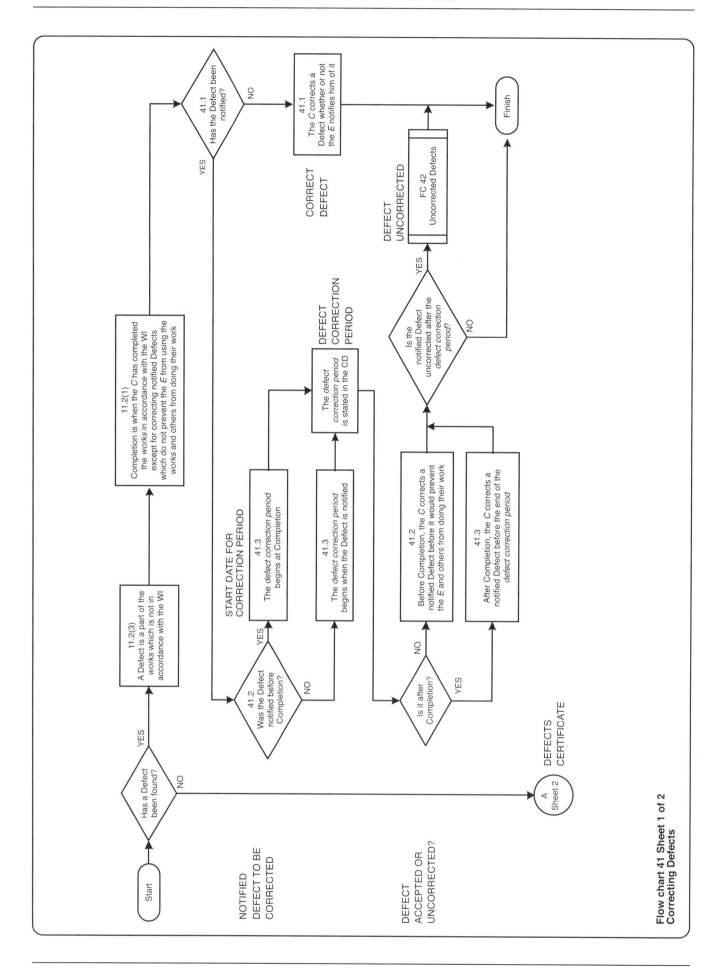

Flow chart 41 Sheet 1 of 2
Correcting Defects

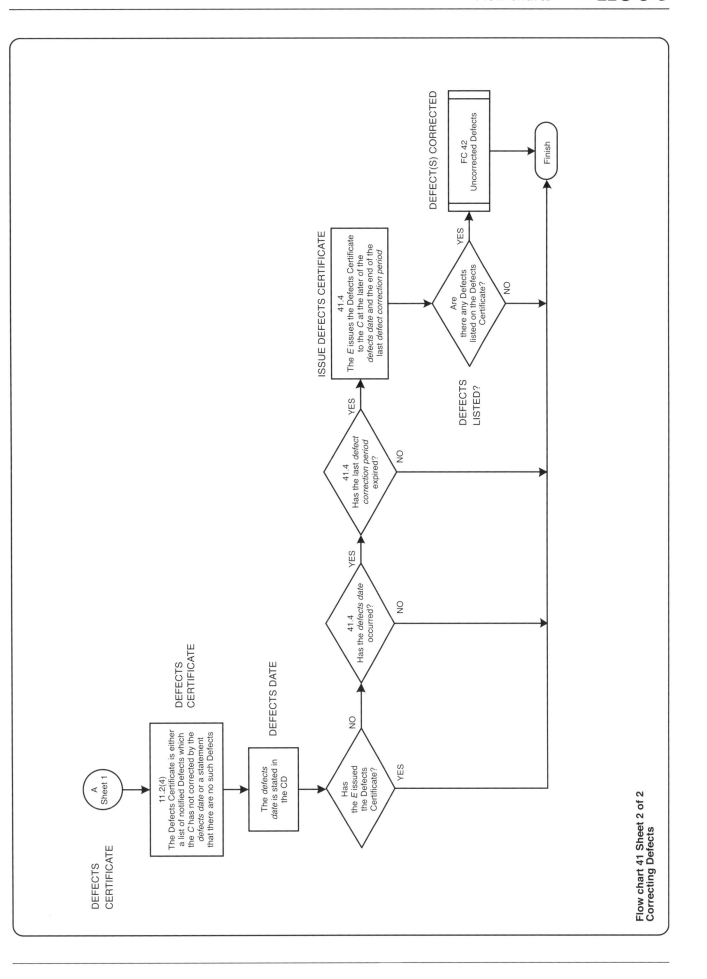

DEFECTS CERTIFICATE

A
Sheet 1

11.2(4)
The Defects Certificate is either a list of notified Defects which the *C* has not corrected by the *defects date* or a statement that there are no such Defects

DEFECTS CERTIFICATE

The *defects date* is stated in the CD

DEFECTS DATE

Has the *E* issued the Defects Certificate?

NO / YES

41.4
Has the *defects date* occurred?

YES / NO

41.4
Has the last *defect correction period* expired?

YES / NO

ISSUE DEFECTS CERTIFICATE

41.4
The *E* issues the Defects Certificate to the *C* at the later of the *defects date* and the end of the last *defect correction period*

DEFECTS LISTED?

Are there any Defects listed on the Defects Certificate?

YES / NO

DEFECT(S) CORRECTED

FC 42
Uncorrected Defects

Finish

Flow chart 41 Sheet 2 of 2
Correcting Defects

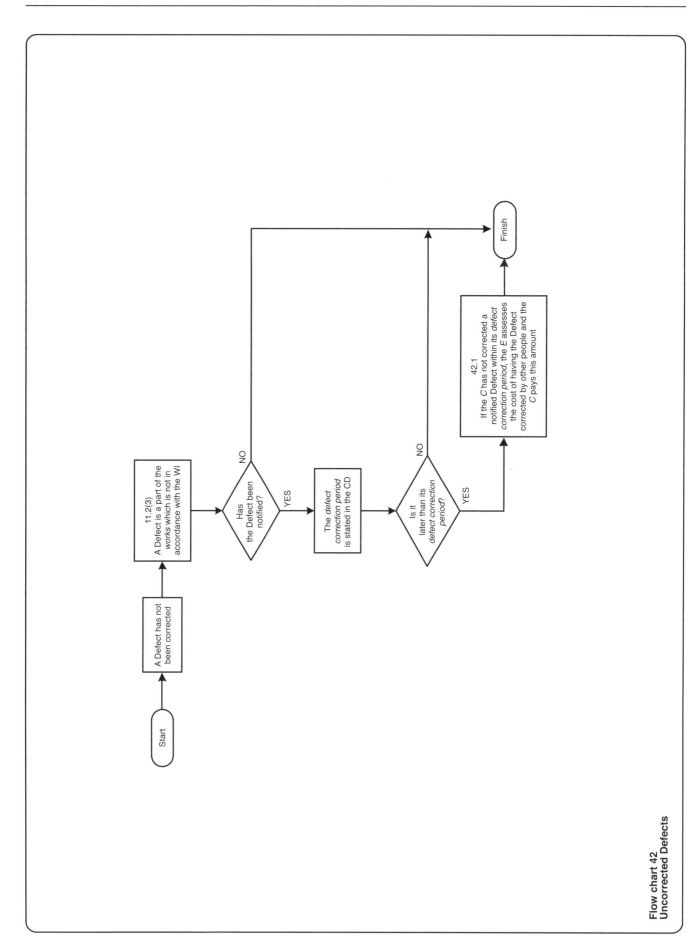

Start

A Defect has not been corrected

11.2(3)
A Defect is a part of the *works* which is not in accordance with the WI

Has the Defect been notified?

NO

YES

The *defect correction period* is stated in the CD

Is it later than its *defect correction period*?

NO

YES

42.1
If the *C* has not corrected a notified Defect within its *defect correction period*, the *E* assesses the cost of having the Defect corrected by other people and the *C* pays this amount

Finish

Flow chart 42
Uncorrected Defects

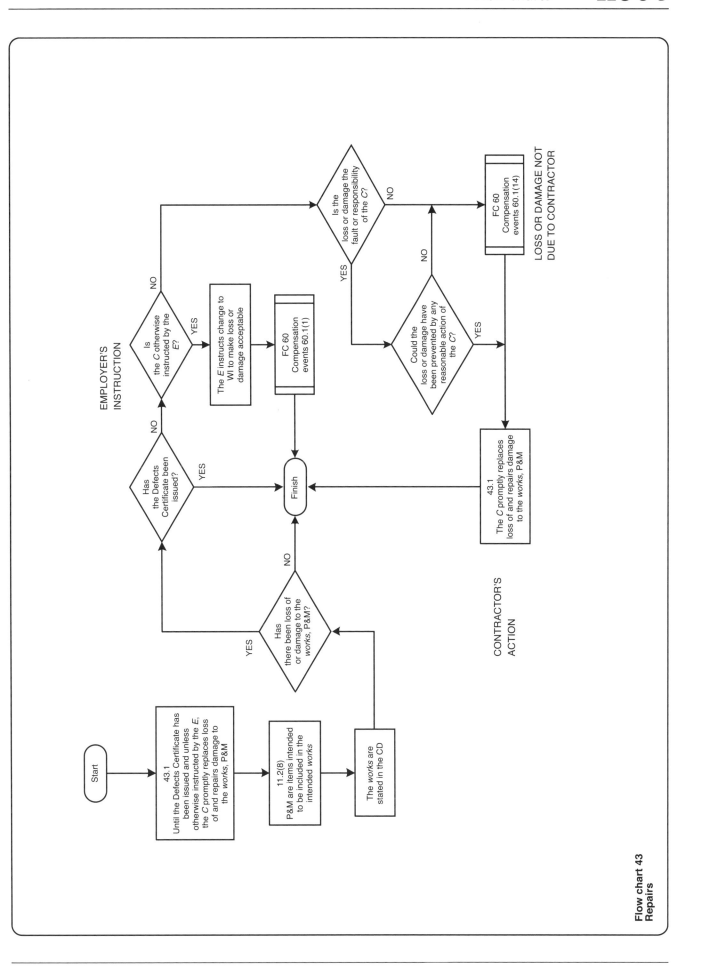

EMPLOYER'S
INSTRUCTION

LOSS OR DAMAGE NOT
DUE TO CONTRACTOR

CONTRACTOR'S
ACTION

Start

43.1
Until the Defects Certificate has been issued and unless otherwise instructed by the *E*, the *C* promptly replaces loss of and repairs damage to the *works*, P&M

11.2(8)
P&M are items intended to be included in the intended *works*

The *works* are stated in the CD

Has there been loss of or damage to the *works*, P&M? — NO → **Finish**
YES

Has the Defects Certificate been issued? — NO → Is the *C* otherwise instructed by the *E*?
YES → **Finish**

Is the *C* otherwise instructed by the *E*? — NO → Is the loss or damage the fault or responsibility of the *C*?
YES ↓

The *E* instructs change to WI to make loss or damage acceptable

FC 60
Compensation events 60.1(1)

Is the loss or damage the fault or responsibility of the *C*? — YES ↓ — NO → FC 60 Compensation events 60.1(14)

Could the loss or damage have been prevented by any reasonable action of the *C*? — NO → FC 60 Compensation events 60.1(14)
YES ↓

43.1
The *C* promptly replaces loss of and repairs damage to the *works*, P&M → **Finish**

Flow chart 43
Repairs

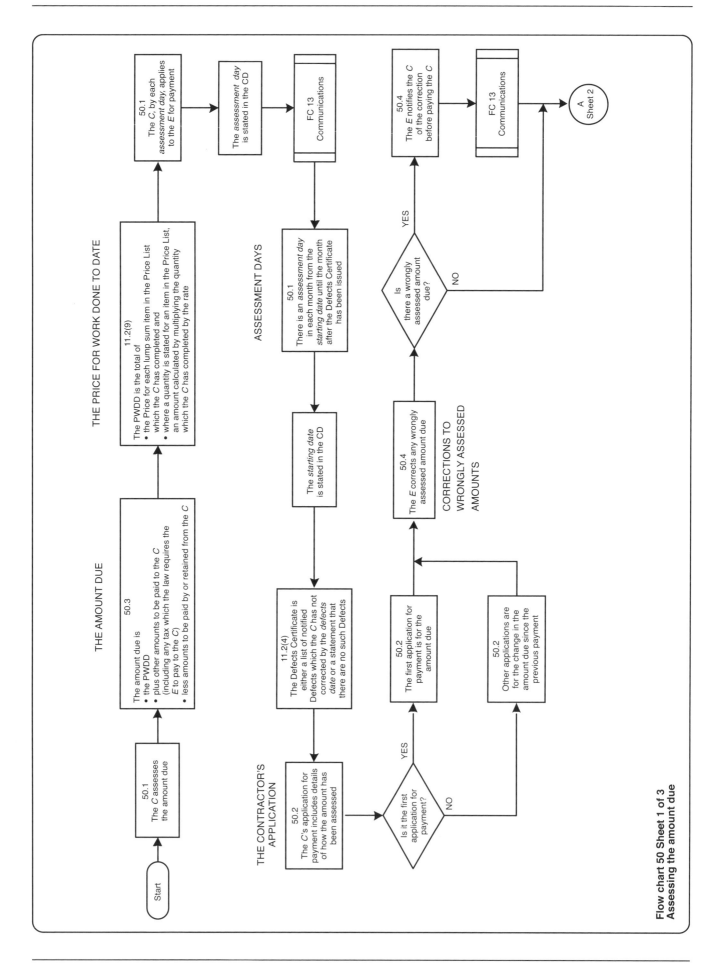

THE PRICE FOR WORK DONE TO DATE

11.2(9)
The PWDD is the total of
• the Price for each lump sum item in the Price List which the C has completed and
• where a quantity is stated for an item in the Price List, an amount calculated by multiplying the quantity which the C has completed by the rate

50.1
The C, by each *assessment day*, applies to the E for payment

The *assessment day* is stated in the CD

FC 13
Communications

ASSESSMENT DAYS

50.1
There is an *assessment day* in each month from the *starting date* until the month after the Defects Certificate has been issued

The *starting date* is stated in the CD

50.4
The E notifies the C of the correction before paying the C

FC 13
Communications

A
Sheet 2

THE AMOUNT DUE

50.3
The amount due is
• the PWDD
• plus other amounts to be paid to the C (including any tax which the law requires the E to pay to the C)
• less amounts to be paid by or retained from the C

50.1
The C assesses the amount due

Start

Is there a wrongly assessed amount due?

YES

NO

50.4
The E corrects any wrongly assessed amount due

CORRECTIONS TO WRONGLY ASSESSED AMOUNTS

THE CONTRACTOR'S APPLICATION

11.2(4)
The Defects Certificate is either a list of notified Defects which the C has not corrected by the *defects date* or a statement that there are no such Defects

50.2
The C's application for payment includes details of how the amount has been assessed

Is it the first application for payment?

YES

NO

50.2
The first application for payment is for the amount due

50.2
Other applications are for the change in the amount due since the previous payment

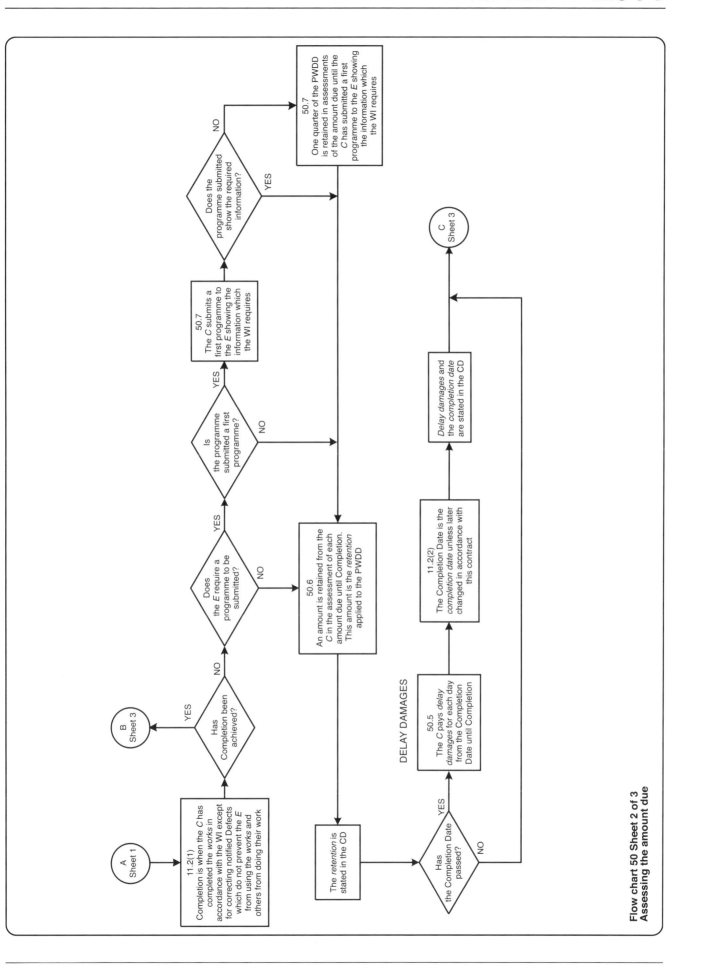

Flow chart 50 Sheet 2 of 3
Assessing the amount due

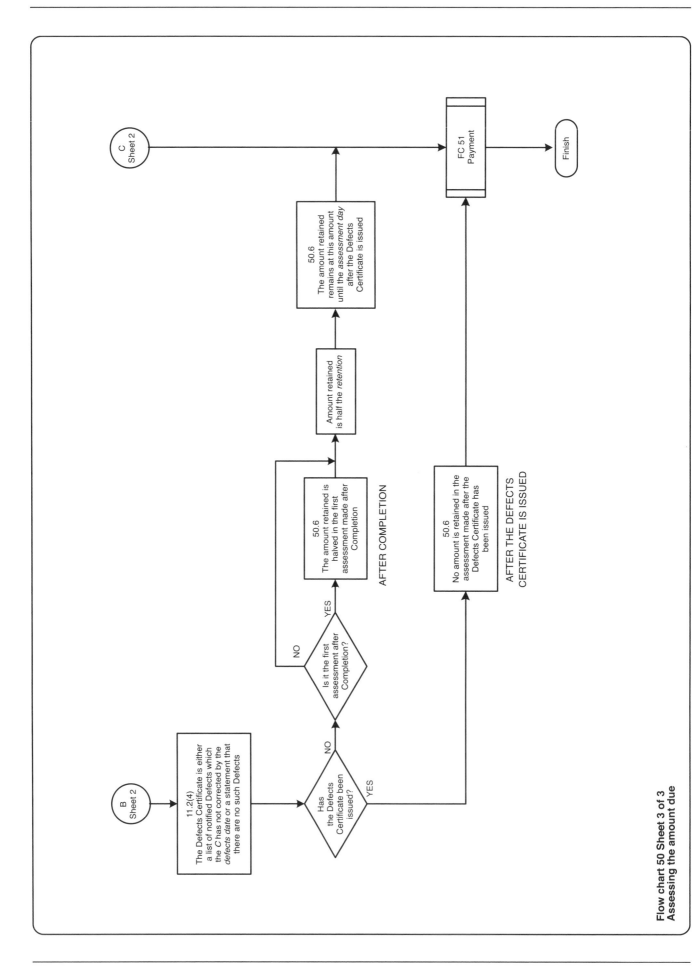

Flow chart 50 Sheet 3 of 3
Assessing the amount due

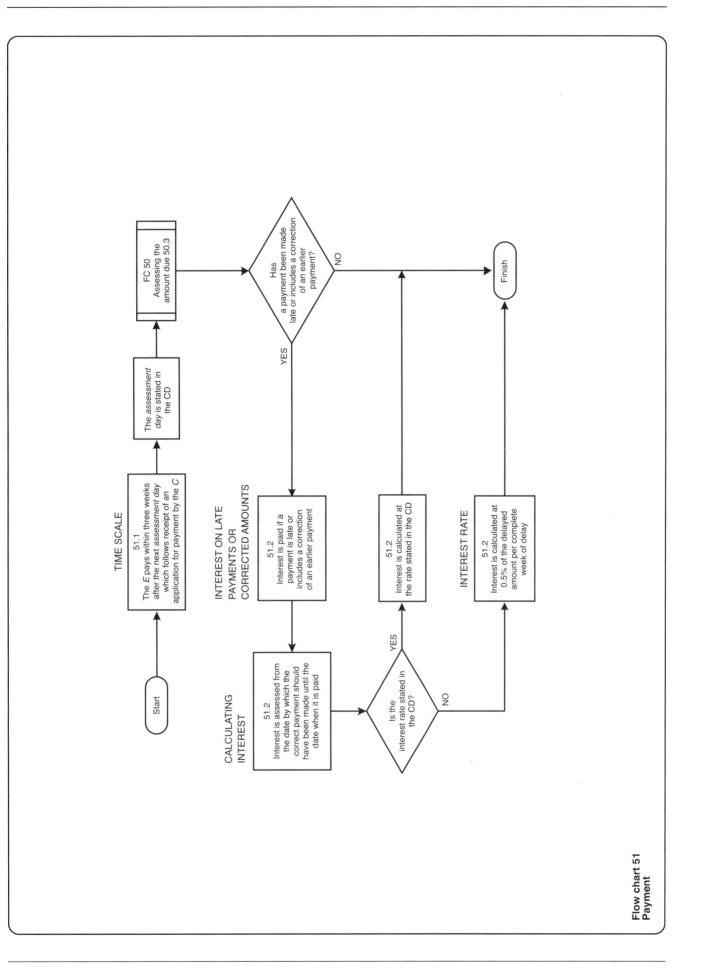

Flow chart 51
Payment

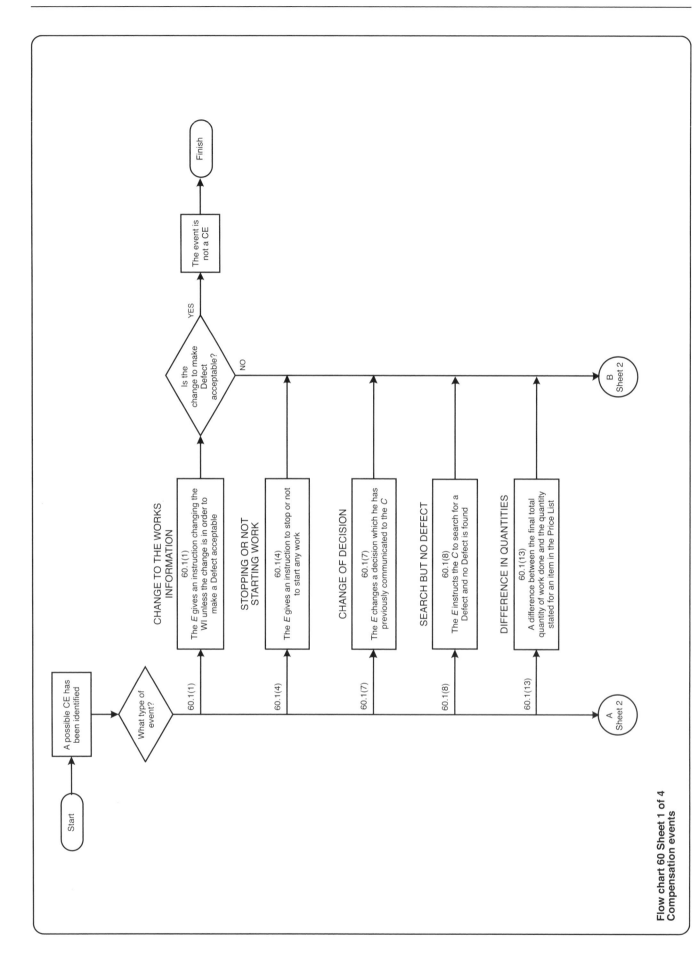

Flow chart 60 Sheet 1 of 4
Compensation events

Start

A possible CE has been identified

What type of event?

CHANGE TO THE WORKS INFORMATION
60.1(1)
The E gives an instruction changing the WI unless the change is in order to make a Defect acceptable
60.1(1)

STOPPING OR NOT STARTING WORK
60.1(4)
The E gives an instruction to stop or not to start any work
60.1(4)

CHANGE OF DECISION
60.1(7)
The E changes a decision which he has previously communicated to the C
60.1(7)

SEARCH BUT NO DEFECT
60.1(8)
The E instructs the C to search for a Defect and no Defect is found
60.1(8)

DIFFERENCE IN QUANTITIES
60.1(13)
A difference between the final total quantity of work done and the quantity stated for an item in the Price List
60.1(13)

Is the change to make Defect acceptable?

YES

The event is not a CE

Finish

NO

B Sheet 2

A Sheet 2

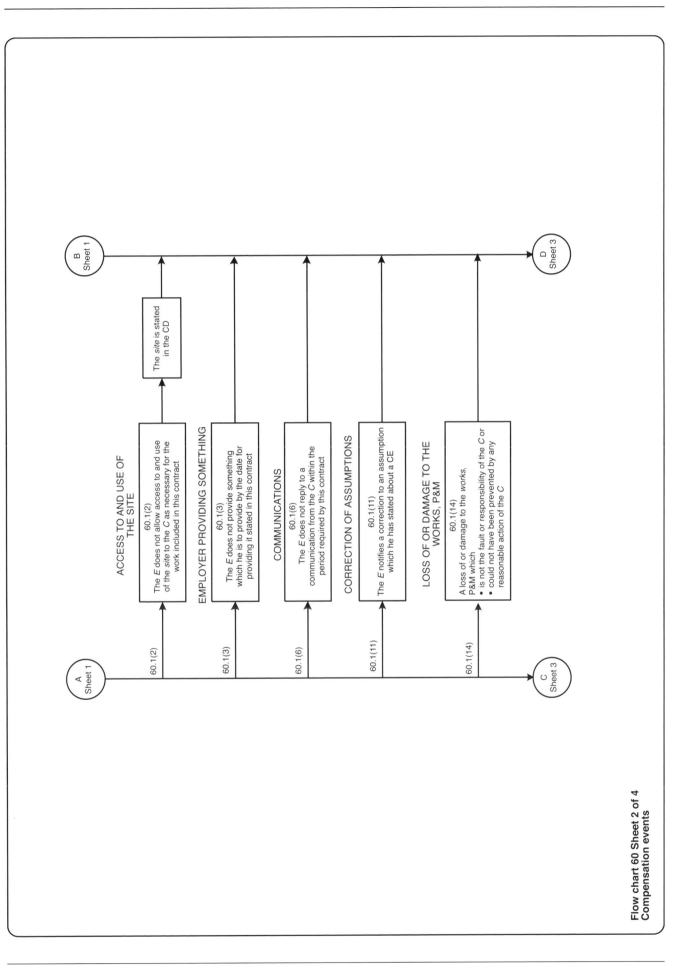

ACCESS TO AND USE OF THE SITE

60.1(2)
The *E* does not allow access to and use of the *site* to the *C* as necessary for the work included in this contract

The *site* is stated in the CD

EMPLOYER PROVIDING SOMETHING

60.1(3)
The *E* does not provide something which he is to provide by the date for providing it stated in this contract

COMMUNICATIONS

60.1(6)
The *E* does not reply to a communication from the *C* within the period required by this contract

CORRECTION OF ASSUMPTIONS

60.1(11)
The *E* notifies a correction to an assumption which he has stated about a CE

LOSS OF OR DAMAGE TO THE WORKS, P&M

60.1(14)
A loss of or damage to the *works*, P&M which
• is not the fault or responsibility of the *C* or
• could not have been prevented by any reasonable action of the *C*

A Sheet 1

60.1(2)

60.1(3)

60.1(6)

60.1(11)

60.1(14)

B Sheet 1

D Sheet 3

C Sheet 3

**Flow chart 60 Sheet 2 of 4
Compensation events**

WEATHER

60.1(10)
The C is prevented by weather from carrying out all work on the site for periods of time, each at least one full working day, which are in total more than one seventh of the total number of days between the starting date and the Completion Date. In assessing this event, only the working days which exceed this limit and on which work is prevented by no other cause are taken into account

Assumptions on Contractor's actions

The site and starting date are stated in the CD

11.2(12)
SI is information which describes the site and its surroundings and is in a document called 'Site Information'

60.2
In judging the physical conditions for the purposes of assessing any CE, the C is assumed to have taken into account
- the SI,
- publicly available information referred to in the SI,
- information obtainable from a visual inspection of the site and
- other information which an experienced contractor could reasonably be expected to have or to obtain

Are the judging criteria in clauses 60.1(9) & 60.2 satisfied? — YES → F Sheet 4

NO

Are the physical conditions within the site? — YES

NO →

Are the physical conditions due to the weather? — YES

NO

PHYSICAL CONDITIONS

60.1(9)
The C encounters physical conditions which
- are within the site,
- are not weather conditions and
- an experienced contractor would have judged, at the date of the C's Offer, to have such a small chance of occurring that it would have been unreasonable to have allowed for them. Only the difference between the physical conditions encountered and those for which it would have been reasonable to have allowed is taken into account in assessing a CE

C Sheet 2

60.1(10)

60.1(9)

D Sheet 2

E Sheet 4

**Flow chart 60 Sheet 3 of 4
Compensation events**

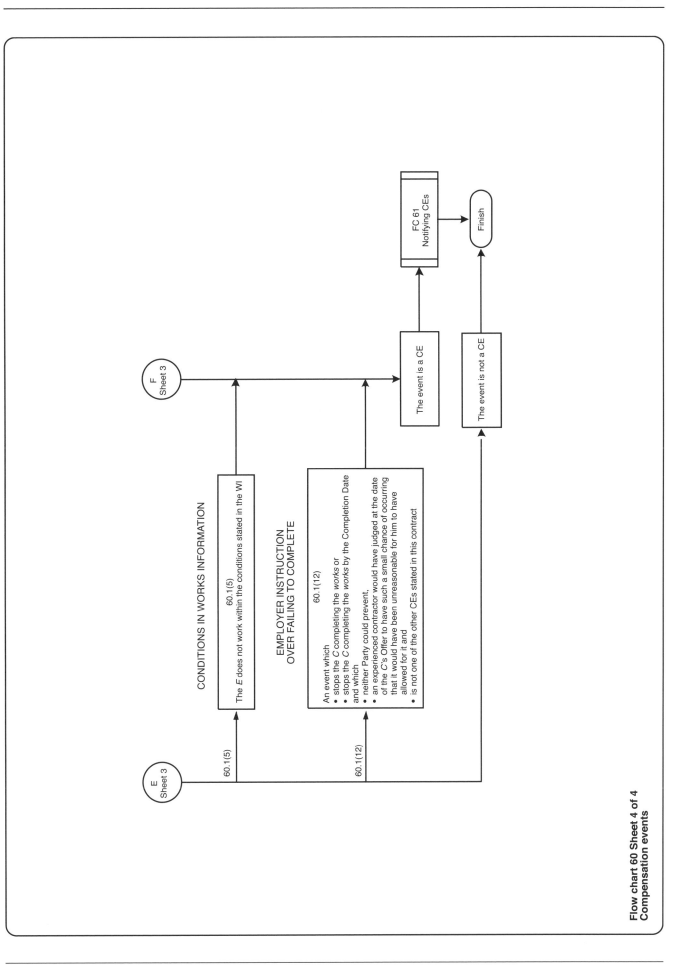

CONDITIONS IN WORKS INFORMATION

60.1(5)

The E does not work within the conditions stated in the WI

EMPLOYER INSTRUCTION
OVER FAILING TO COMPLETE

60.1(12)

An event which
• stops the C completing the works or
• stops the C completing the works by the Completion Date
and which
• neither Party could prevent,
• an experienced contractor would have judged at the date
  of the C's Offer to have such a small chance of occurring
  that it would have been unreasonable for him to have
  allowed for it and
• is not one of the other CEs stated in this contract

The event is a CE

The event is not a CE

FC 61
Notifying CEs

Finish

F
Sheet 3

E
Sheet 3

60.1(5)

60.1(12)

Flow chart 60 Sheet 4 of 4
Compensation events

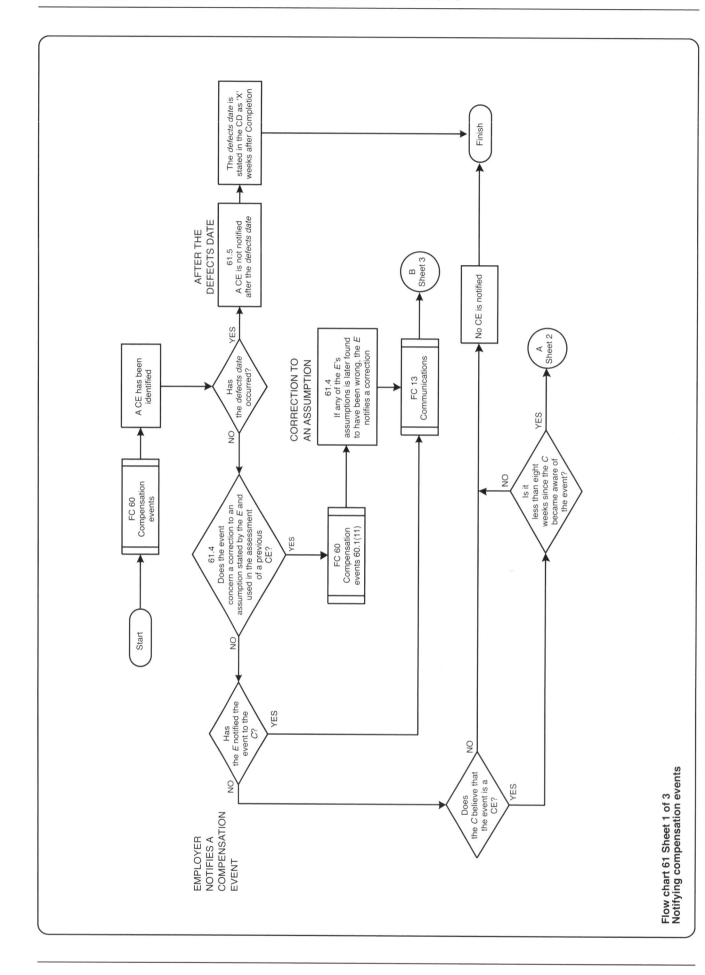

EMPLOYER
NOTIFIES A
COMPENSATION
EVENT

Start

FC 60
Compensation
events

A CE has been
identified

61.4
Does the event
concern a correction to an
assumption stated by the E and
used in the assessment
of a previous
CE?

NO

YES

Has
the defects date
occurred?

NO

YES

AFTER THE
DEFECTS DATE

61.5
A CE is not notified
after the defects date

The defects date is
stated in the CD as 'X'
weeks after Completion

Finish

FC 60
Compensation
events 60.1(11)

CORRECTION TO
AN ASSUMPTION

61.4
If any of the E's
assumptions is later found
to have been wrong, the E
notifies a correction

FC 13
Communications

B
Sheet 3

Has
the E notified the
event to the
C?

NO

YES

No CE is notified

Is it
less than eight
weeks since the C
became aware of
the event?

YES

NO

A
Sheet 2

Does
the C believe that
the event is a
CE?

NO

YES

Flow chart 61 Sheet 1 of 3
Notifying compensation events

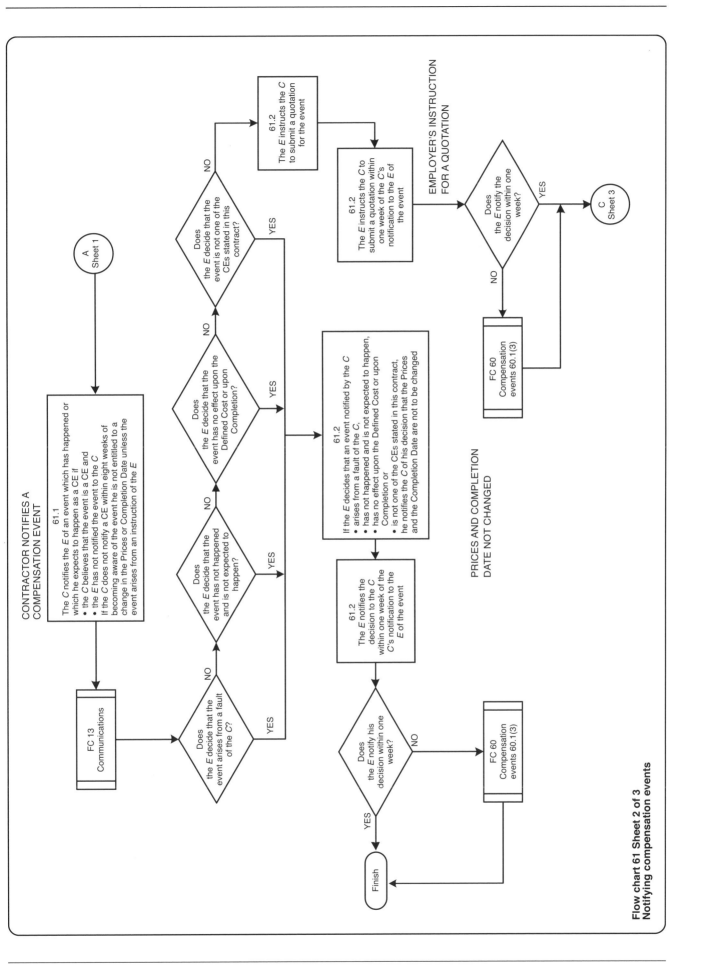

CONTRACTOR NOTIFIES A
COMPENSATION EVENT

61.1
The C notifies the E of an event which has happened or
which he expects to happen as a CE if
• the C believes that the event is a CE and
• the E has not notified the event to the C
If the C does not notify a CE within eight weeks of
becoming aware of the event he is not entitled to a
change in the Prices or Completion Date unless the
event arises from an instruction of the E

A
Sheet 1

FC 13
Communications

Does
the E decide that the
event arises from a fault
of the C?

NO

YES

Does
the E decide that the
event has not happened
and is not expected to
happen?

NO

YES

Does
the E decide that the
event has no effect upon the
Defined Cost or upon
Completion?

NO

YES

Does
the E decide that the
event is not one of the
CEs stated in this
contract?

NO

YES

61.2
The E instructs the C
to submit a quotation
for the event

61.2
The E instructs the C to
submit a quotation within
one week of the C's
notification to the E of
the event

EMPLOYER'S INSTRUCTION
FOR A QUOTATION

Does
the E notify the
decision within one
week?

YES

NO

C
Sheet 3

FC 60
Compensation
events 60.1(3)

61.2
If the E decides that an event notified by the C
• arises from a fault of the C,
• has not happened and is not expected to happen,
• has no effect upon the Defined Cost or upon
  Completion or
• is not one of the CEs stated in this contract,
he notifies the C of his decision that the Prices
and the Completion Date are not to be changed

61.2
The E notifies the
decision to the C
within one week of the
C's notification to the
E of the event

PRICES AND COMPLETION
DATE NOT CHANGED

Does
the E notify his
decision within one
week?

YES

NO

FC 60
Compensation
events 60.1(3)

Finish

Flow chart 61 Sheet 2 of 3
Notifying compensation events

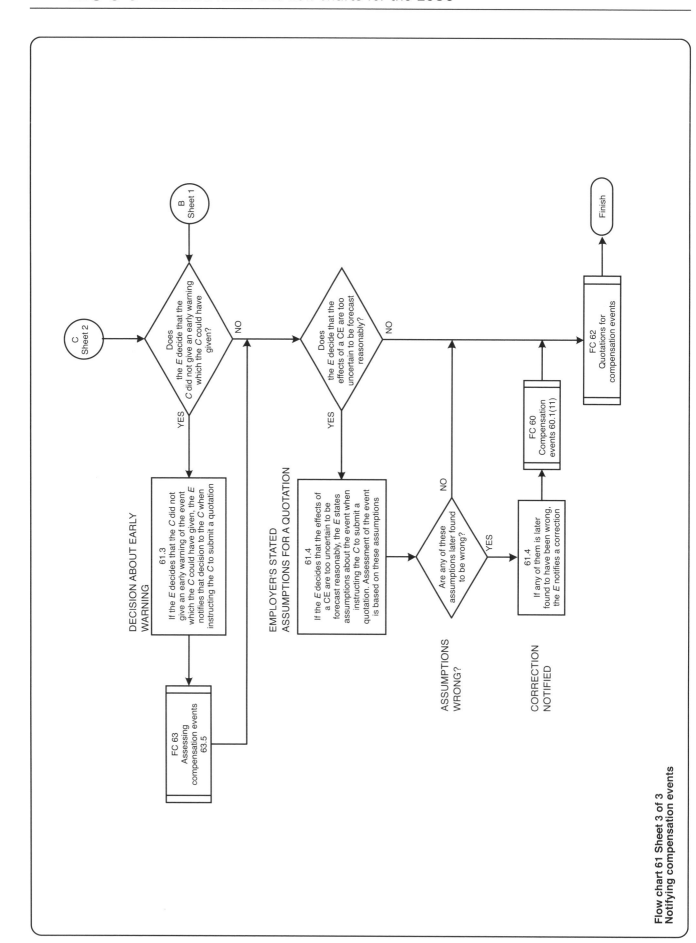

DECISION ABOUT EARLY WARNING

61.3

If the *E* decides that the *C* did not give an early warning of the event which the *C* could have given, the *E* notifies that decision to the *C* when instructing the *C* to submit a quotation

Does the *E* decide that the *C* did not give an early warning which the *C* could have given?

YES / NO

C Sheet 2

B Sheet 1

FC 63 Assessing compensation events 63.5

EMPLOYER'S STATED ASSUMPTIONS FOR A QUOTATION

61.4

If the *E* decides that the effects of a CE are too uncertain to be forecast reasonably, the *E* states assumptions about the event when instructing the *C* to submit a quotation. Assessment of the event is based on these assumptions

Does the *E* decide that the effects of a CE are too uncertain to be forecast reasonably?

YES / NO

ASSUMPTIONS WRONG?

Are any of these assumptions later found to be wrong?

NO / YES

CORRECTION NOTIFIED

61.4

If any of them is later found to have been wrong, the *E* notifies a correction

FC 60 Compensation events 60.1(11)

FC 62 Quotations for compensation events

Finish

Flow chart 61 Sheet 3 of 3
Notifying compensation events

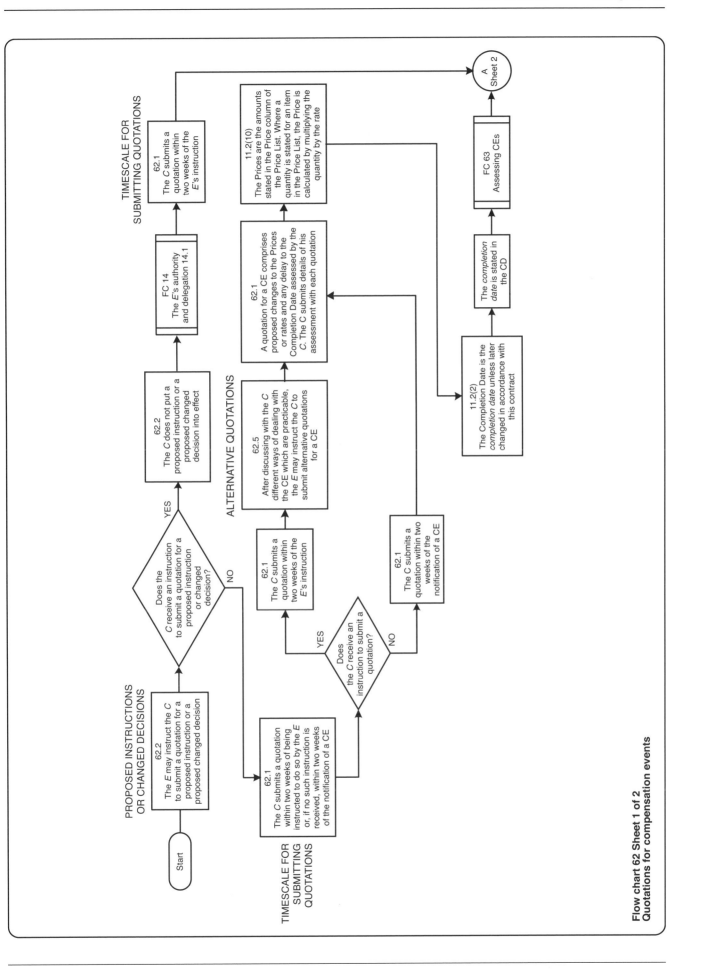

TIMESCALE FOR SUBMITTING QUOTATIONS

62.1
The *C* submits a quotation within two weeks of the *E*'s instruction

11.2(10)
The Prices are the amounts stated in the Price column of the Price List. Where a quantity is stated for an item in the Price List, the Price is calculated by multiplying the quantity by the rate

A
Sheet 2

FC 14
The *E*'s authority and delegation 14.1

FC 63
Assessing CEs

PROPOSED INSTRUCTIONS OR CHANGED DECISIONS

62.2
The *C* does not put a proposed instruction or a proposed changed decision into effect

62.1
A quotation for a CE comprises proposed changes to the Prices or rates and any delay to the Completion Date assessed by the *C*. The *C* submits details of his assessment with each quotation

The *completion date* is stated in the CD

Does the *C* receive an instruction to submit a quotation for a proposed instruction or changed decision?

YES

NO

ALTERNATIVE QUOTATIONS

62.5
After discussing with the *C* different ways of dealing with the CE which are practicable, the *E* may instruct the *C* to submit alternative quotations for a CE

11.2(2)
The Completion Date is the *completion date* unless later changed in accordance with this contract

62.2
The *E* may instruct the *C* to submit a quotation for a proposed instruction or a proposed changed decision

62.1
The *C* submits a quotation within two weeks of the *E*'s instruction

62.1
The *C* submits a quotation within two weeks of the notification of a CE

Does the *C* receive an instruction to submit a quotation?

YES

NO

Start

TIMESCALE FOR SUBMITTING QUOTATIONS

62.1
The *C* submits a quotation within two weeks of being instructed to do so by the *E* or, if no such instruction is received, within two weeks of the notification of a CE

Flow chart 62 Sheet 1 of 2
Quotations for compensation events

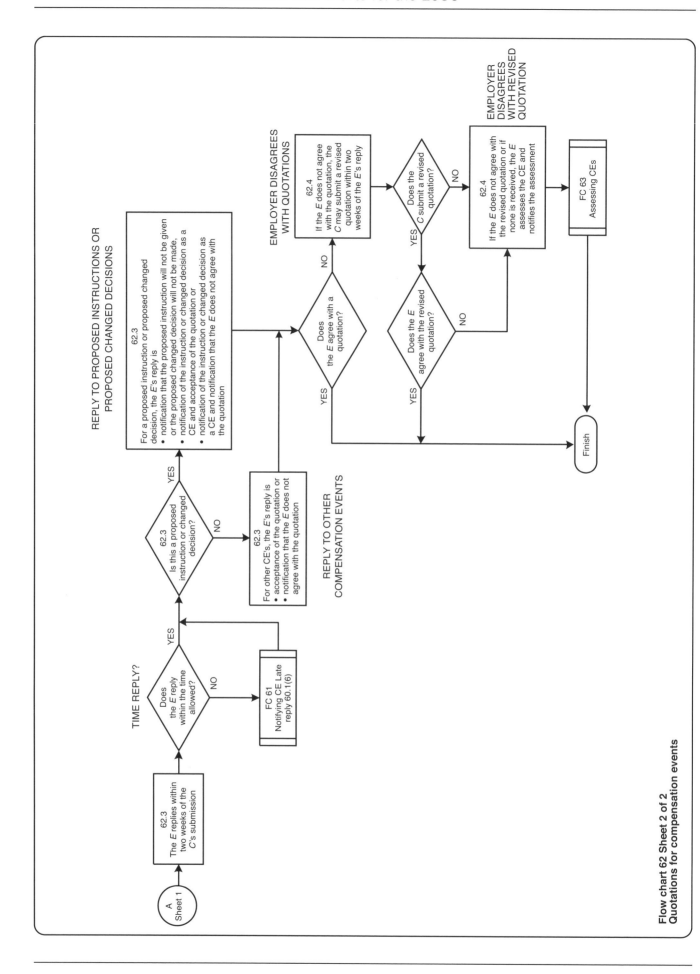

TIME REPLY?

A Sheet 1

62.3
The E replies within two weeks of the C's submission

Does the E reply within the time allowed?

NO → FC 61 Notifying CE Late reply 60.1(6)

YES

62.3
Is this a proposed instruction or changed decision?

NO → 62.3
For other CE's, the E's reply is
• acceptance of the quotation or
• notification that the E does not agree with the quotation

REPLY TO OTHER COMPENSATION EVENTS

YES

REPLY TO PROPOSED INSTRUCTIONS OR PROPOSED CHANGED DECISIONS

62.3
For a proposed instruction or proposed changed decision, the E's reply is
• notification that the proposed instruction will not be given or the proposed changed decision will not be made,
• notification of the instruction or changed decision as a CE and acceptance of the quotation or
• notification of the instruction or changed decision as a CE and notification that the E does not agree with the quotation

Does the E agree with a quotation?

NO → **EMPLOYER DISAGREES WITH QUOTATIONS**

62.4
If the E does not agree with the quotation, the C may submit a revised quotation within two weeks of the E's reply

Does the C submit a revised quotation?

NO → 62.4
If the E does not agree with the revised quotation or if none is received, the E assesses the CE and notifies the assessment → **EMPLOYER DISAGREES WITH REVISED QUOTATION**

YES

Does the E agree with the revised quotation?

YES

NO → 62.4
If the E does not agree with the revised quotation or if none is received, the E assesses the CE and notifies the assessment

YES

FC 63
Assessing CEs

Finish

Flow chart 62 Sheet 2 of 2
Quotations for compensation events

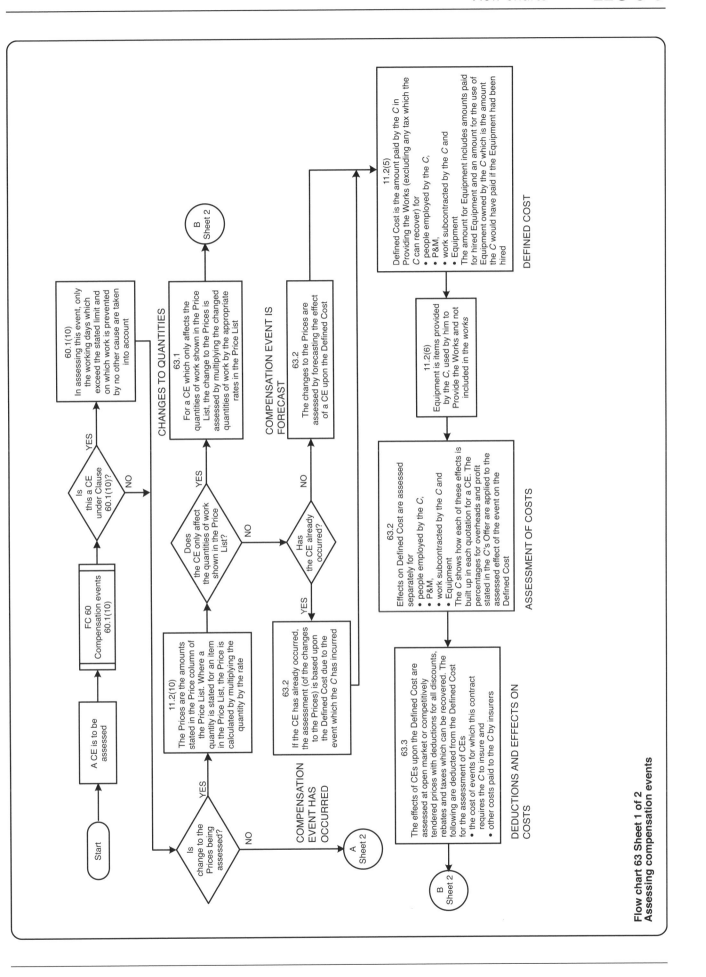

Flow chart 63 Sheet 1 of 2
Assessing compensation events

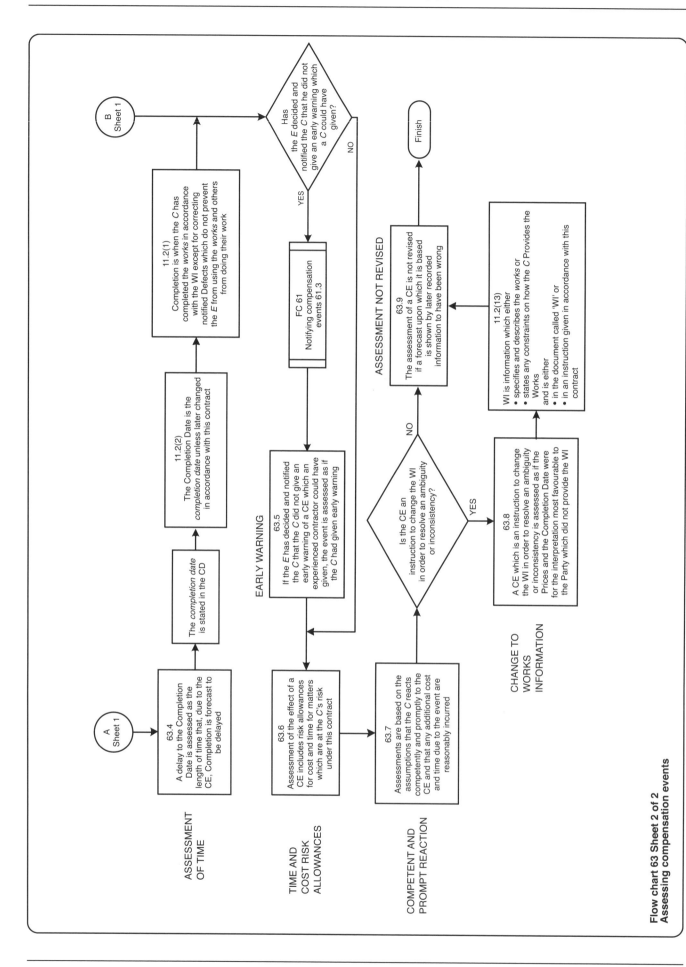
B
Sheet 1

Has the *E* decided and notified the *C* that he did not give an early warning which a *C* could have given?

YES → FC 61
Notifying compensation events 61.3

NO

11.2(1)
Completion is when the *C* has completed the *works* in accordance with the WI except for correcting notified Defects which do not prevent the *E* from using the *works* and others from doing their work

11.2(2)
The Completion Date is the *completion date* unless later changed in accordance with this contract

The *completion date* is stated in the CD

A
Sheet 1

ASSESSMENT OF TIME

63.4
A delay to the Completion Date is assessed as the length of time that, due to the CE, Completion is forecast to be delayed

EARLY WARNING

63.5
If the *E* has decided and notified the *C* that the *C* did not give an early warning of a CE which an experienced contractor could have given, the event is assessed as if the *C* had given early warning

TIME AND COST RISK ALLOWANCES

63.6
Assessment of the effect of a CE includes risk allowances for cost and time for matters which are at the *C*'s risk under this contract

COMPETENT AND PROMPT REACTION

63.7
Assessments are based on the assumptions that the *C* reacts competently and promptly to the CE and that any additional cost and time due to the event are reasonably incurred

ASSESSMENT NOT REVISED

63.9
The assessment of a CE is not revised if a forecast upon which it is based is shown by later recorded information to have been wrong

Finish

Is the CE an instruction to change the WI in order to resolve an ambiguity or inconsistency?

NO

YES

CHANGE TO WORKS INFORMATION

63.8
A CE which is an instruction to change the WI in order to resolve an ambiguity or inconsistency is assessed as if the Prices and the Completion Date were for the interpretation most favourable to the Party which did not provide the WI

11.2(13)
WI is information which either
• specifies and describes the *works* or
• states any constraints on how the *C* Provides the Works
and is either
• in the document called 'WI' or
• in an instruction given in accordance with this contract

Flow chart 63 Sheet 2 of 2
Assessing compensation events

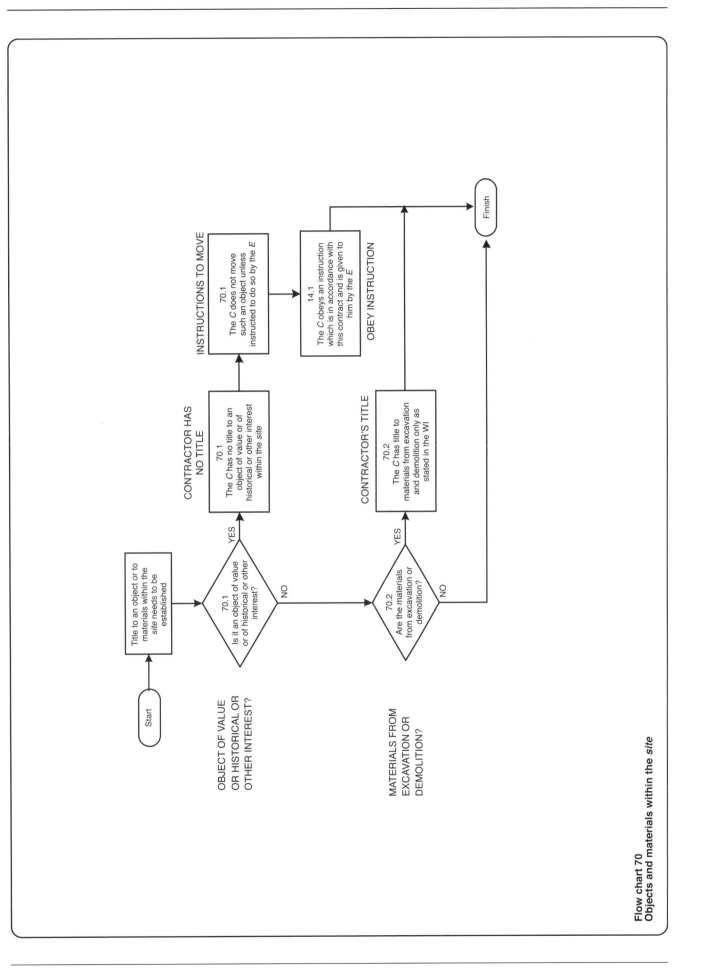

**OBJECT OF VALUE
OR HISTORICAL OR
OTHER INTEREST?**

**CONTRACTOR HAS
NO TITLE**

INSTRUCTIONS TO MOVE

OBEY INSTRUCTION

**MATERIALS FROM
EXCAVATION OR
DEMOLITION?**

CONTRACTOR'S TITLE

Start

Title to an object or to
materials within the
site needs to be
established

70.1
Is it an object of value
or of historical or other
interest?

YES

70.1
The *C* has no title to an
object of value or of
historical or other interest
within the *site*

70.1
The *C* does not move
such an object unless
instructed to do so by the *E*

14.1
The *C* obeys an instruction
which is in accordance with
this contract and is given to
him by the *E*

NO

70.2
Are the materials
from excavation or
demolition?

YES

70.2
The *C* has title to
materials from excavation
and demolition only as
stated in the WI

NO

Finish

**Flow chart 70
Objects and materials within the *site***

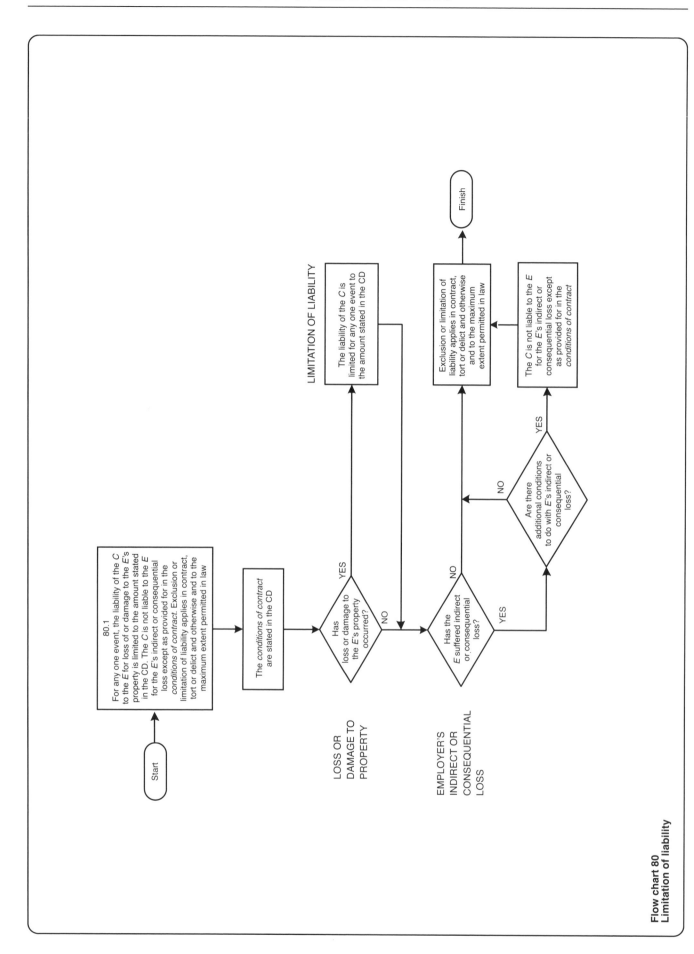

LIMITATION OF LIABILITY

Start

80.1
For any one event, the liability of the *C* to the *E* for loss of or damage to the *E*'s property is limited to the amount stated in the CD. The *C* is not liable to the *E* for the *E*'s indirect or consequential loss except as provided for in the *conditions of contract*. Exclusion or limitation of liability applies in contract, tort or delict and otherwise and to the maximum extent permitted in law

The *conditions of contract* are stated in the CD

LOSS OR DAMAGE TO PROPERTY

Has loss or damage to the *E*'s property occurred? — YES → The liability of the *C* is limited for any one event to the amount stated in the CD

NO

EMPLOYER'S INDIRECT OR CONSEQUENTIAL LOSS

Has the *E* suffered indirect or consequential loss? — NO → Exclusion or limitation of liability applies in contract, tort or delict and otherwise and to the maximum extent permitted in law → Finish

YES

Are there additional conditions to do with *E*'s indirect or consequential loss? — YES → The *C* is not liable to the *E* for the *E*'s indirect or consequential loss except as provided for in the *conditions of contract*

NO

**Flow chart 80
Limitation of liability**

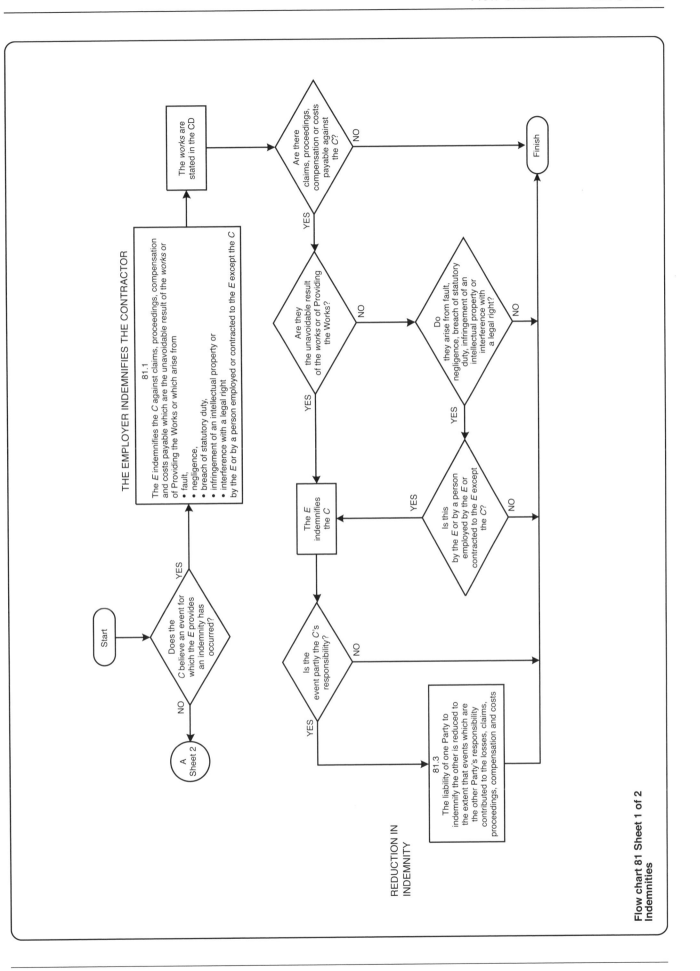

THE EMPLOYER INDEMNIFIES THE CONTRACTOR

Start

Does the C believe an event for which the E provides an indemnity has occurred?

NO → A Sheet 2

YES →

81.1
The E indemnifies the C against claims, proceedings, compensation and costs payable which are the unavoidable result of the works or of Providing the Works or which arise from
- fault,
- negligence,
- breach of statutory duty,
- infringement of an intellectual property or
- interference with a legal right
by the E or by a person employed or contracted to the E except the C

The works are stated in the CD

Are there claims, proceedings, compensation or costs payable against the C?

NO → Finish

YES →

Are they the unavoidable result of the works or of Providing the Works?

YES → The E indemnifies the C

NO →

Do they arise from fault, negligence, breach of statutory duty, infringement of an intellectual property or interference with a legal right?

YES →

Is this by the E or by a person employed by the E or contracted to the E except the C?

YES → The E indemnifies the C

NO →

NO →

Is the event partly the C's responsibility?

YES →

NO →

81.3
The liability of one Party to indemnify the other is reduced to the extent that events which are the other Party's responsibility contributed to the losses, claims, proceedings, compensation and costs

REDUCTION IN INDEMNITY

Flow chart 81 Sheet 1 of 2
Indemnities

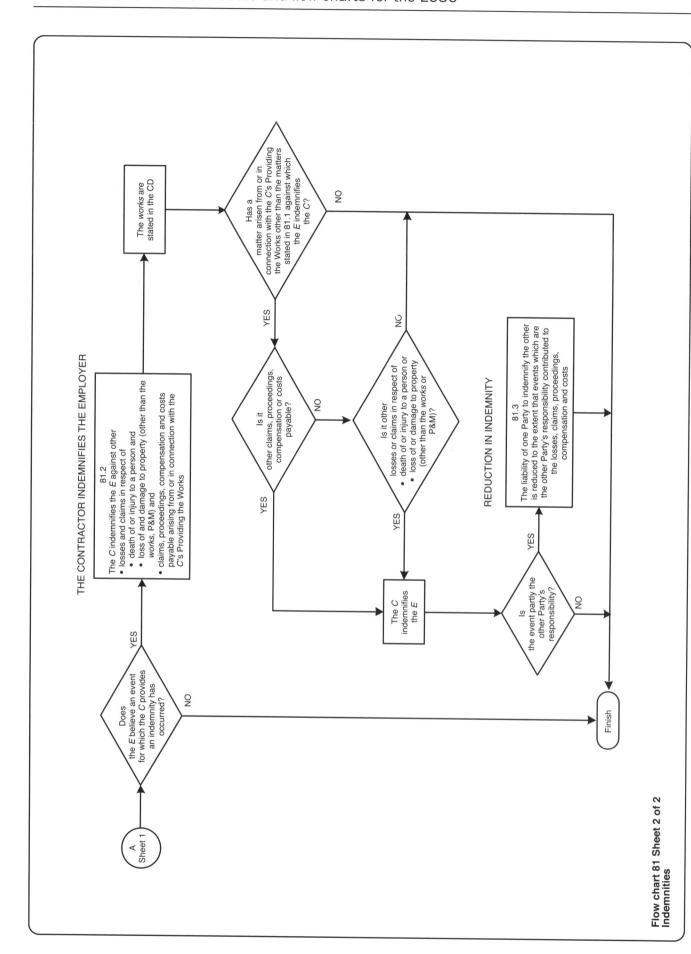

THE CONTRACTOR INDEMNIFIES THE EMPLOYER

A Sheet 1

Does the *E* believe an event for which the *C* provides an indemnity has occurred?

YES →

81.2
The *C* indemnifies the *E* against other
• losses and claims in respect of
  • death of or injury to a person and
  • loss of and damage to property (other than the *works*, P&M) and
• claims, proceedings, compensation and costs payable arising from or in connection with the *C's* Providing the Works

The *works* are stated in the CD

Has a matter arisen from or in connection with the *C's* Providing the Works other than the matters stated in 81.1 against which the *E* indemnifies the *C?*

YES / **NO**

Is it other claims, proceedings, compensation or costs payable?

YES / **NO**

Is it other losses or claims in respect of
• death of or injury to a person or
• loss of or damage to property (other than the *works* or P&M)?

NO / **YES**

The *C* indemnifies the *E*

REDUCTION IN INDEMNITY

81.3
The liability of one Party to indemnify the other is reduced to the extent that events which are the other Party's responsibility contributed to the losses, claims, proceedings, compensation and costs

Is the event partly the other Party's responsibility?

YES / **NO**

Finish

**Flow chart 81 Sheet 2 of 2
Indemnities**

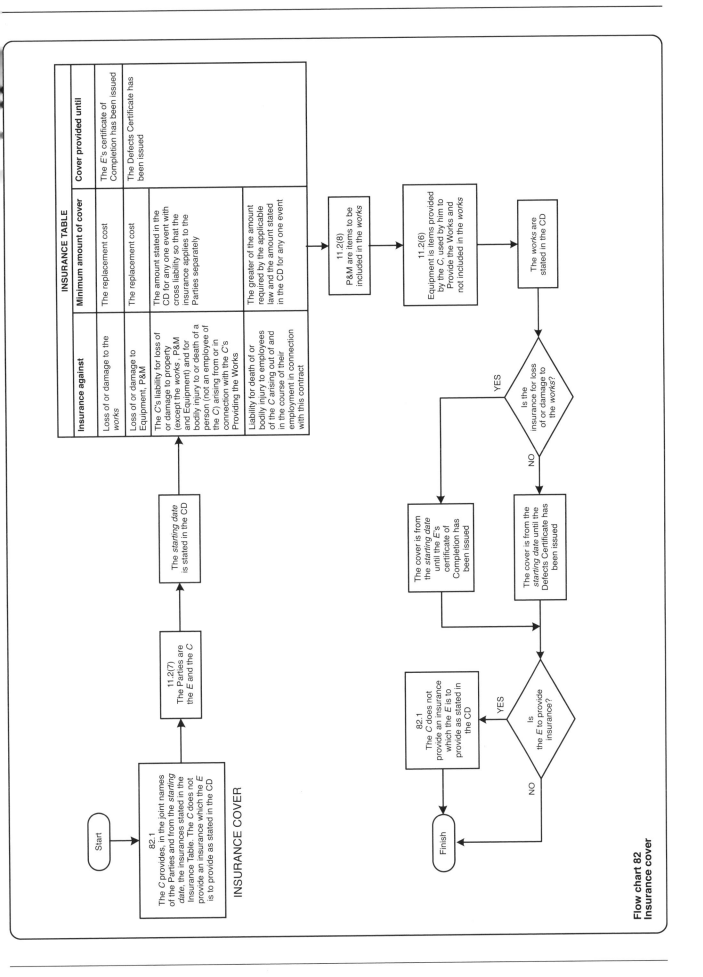

INSURANCE TABLE

Insurance against	Minimum amount of cover	Cover provided until
Loss of or damage to the *works*	The replacement cost	The *E*'s certificate of Completion has been issued
Loss of or damage to Equipment, P&M	The replacement cost	The Defects Certificate has been issued
The *C*'s liability for loss of or damage to property (except the *works* , P&M and Equipment) and for bodily injury to or death of a person (not an employee of the *C*) arising from or in connection with the *C*'s Providing the Works	The amount stated in the CD for any one event with cross liability so that the insurance applies to the Parties separately	
Liability for death of or bodily injury to employees of the *C* arising out of and in the course of their employment in connection with this contract	The greater of the amount required by the applicable law and the amount stated in the CD for any one event	

11.2(8)
P&M are items to be included in the *works*

11.2(6)
Equipment is items provided by the *C*, used by him to Provide the Works and not included in the *works*

The *works* are stated in the CD

11.2(7)
The Parties are the *E* and the *C*

The *starting date* is stated in the CD

INSURANCE COVER

Start

82.1
The *C* provides, in the joint names of the Parties and from the *starting date*, the insurances stated in the Insurance Table. The *C* does not provide an insurance which the *E* is to provide as stated in the CD

Is the insurance for loss of or damage to the *works*?

YES → The cover is from the *starting date* until the *E*'s certificate of Completion has been issued

NO → The cover is from the *starting date* until the Defects Certificate has been issued

Is the *E* to provide insurance?

YES → **82.1**
The *C* does not provide an insurance which the *E* is to provide as stated in the CD

NO → Finish

Flow chart 82
Insurance cover

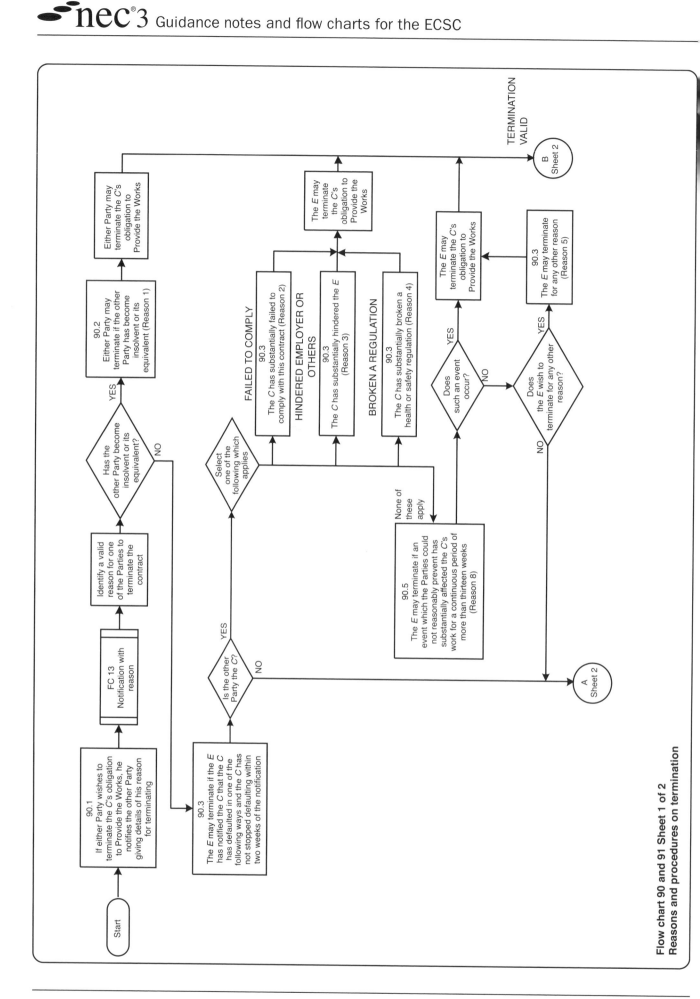

Flow chart 90 and 91 Sheet 1 of 2
Reasons and procedures on termination

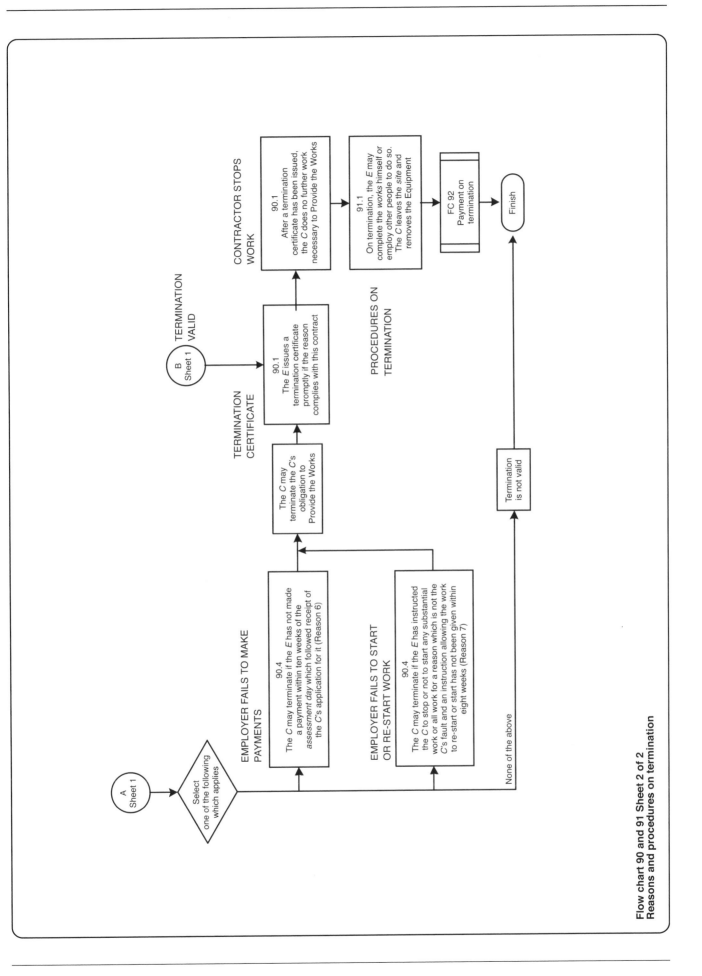

EMPLOYER FAILS TO MAKE PAYMENTS

90.4
The *C* may terminate if the *E* has not made a payment within ten weeks of the *assessment day* which followed receipt of the *C*'s application for it (Reason 6)

EMPLOYER FAILS TO START OR RE-START WORK

90.4
The *C* may terminate if the *E* has instructed the *C* to stop or not to start any substantial work or all work for a reason which is not the *C*'s fault and an instruction allowing the work to re-start or start has not been given within eight weeks (Reason 7)

None of the above

A
Sheet 1

Select one of the following which applies

TERMINATION CERTIFICATE

The *C* may terminate the *C*'s obligation to Provide the Works

90.1
The *E* issues a termination certificate promptly if the reason complies with this contract

B
Sheet 1

TERMINATION VALID

CONTRACTOR STOPS WORK

90.1
After a termination certificate has been issued, the *C* does no further work necessary to Provide the Works

91.1
On termination, the *E* may complete the *works* himself or employ other people to do so. The *C* leaves the *site* and removes the Equipment

PROCEDURES ON TERMINATION

FC 92
Payment on termination

Finish

Termination is not valid

Flow chart 90 and 91 Sheet 2 of 2
Reasons and procedures on termination

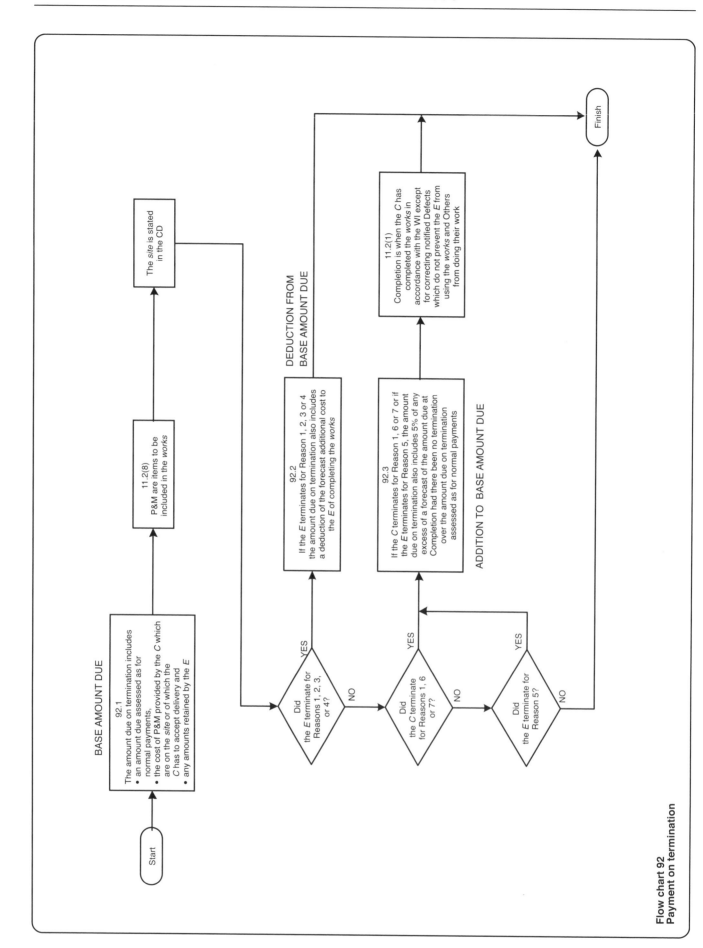

BASE AMOUNT DUE

92.1
The amount due on termination includes
- an amount due assessed as for normal payments,
- the cost of P&M provided by the *C* which are on the *site* or of which the *C* has to accept delivery and
- any amounts retained by the *E*

11.2(8)
P&M are items to be included in the *works*

The *site* is stated in the CD

Start

Did the *E* terminate for Reasons 1, 2, 3, or 4? —— YES

DEDUCTION FROM BASE AMOUNT DUE

92.2
If the *E* terminates for Reason 1, 2, 3 or 4 the amount due on termination also includes a deduction of the forecast additional cost to the *E* of completing the *works*

Did the *C* terminate for Reasons 1, 6 or 7? —— YES

92.3
If the *C* terminates for Reason 1, 6 or 7 or if the *E* terminates for Reason 5, the amount due on termination also includes 5% of any excess of a forecast of the amount due at Completion had there been no termination over the amount due on termination assessed as for normal payments

ADDITION TO BASE AMOUNT DUE

Did the *E* terminate for Reason 5? —— YES

11.2(1)
Completion is when the *C* has completed the *works* in accordance with the WI except for correcting notified Defects which do not prevent the *E* from using the *works* and Others from doing their work

Finish

Flow chart 92
Payment on termination

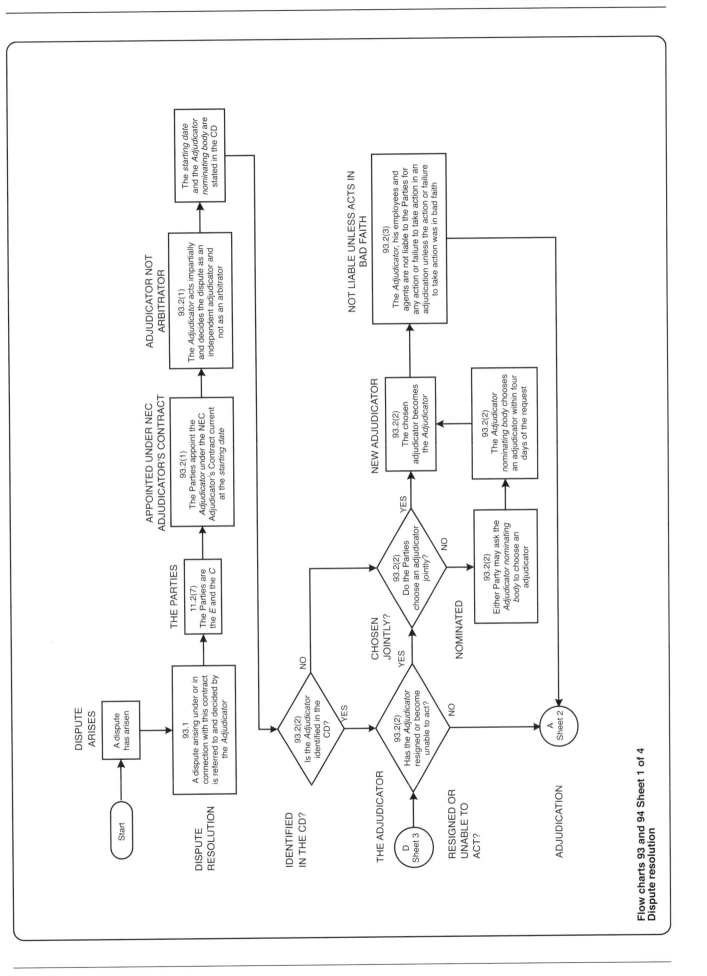

DISPUTE ARISES

Start

A dispute has arisen

DISPUTE RESOLUTION

93.1
A dispute arising under or in connection with this contract is referred to and decided by the *Adjudicator*

THE PARTIES

11.2(7)
The *Parties* are the *E* and the *C*

APPOINTED UNDER NEC ADJUDICATOR'S CONTRACT

93.2(1)
The *Parties* appoint the *Adjudicator* under the NEC Adjudicator's Contract current at the *starting date*

ADJUDICATOR NOT ARBITRATOR

93.2(1)
The *Adjudicator* acts impartially and decides the dispute as an independent adjudicator and not as an arbitrator

The *starting date* and the *Adjudicator nominating body* are stated in the CD

IDENTIFIED IN THE CD?

93.2(2)
Is the *Adjudicator* identified in the CD?

NO / YES

THE ADJUDICATOR

D
Sheet 3

RESIGNED OR UNABLE TO ACT?

93.2(2)
Has the *Adjudicator* resigned or become unable to act?

YES / NO

CHOSEN JOINTLY?

93.2(2)
Do the *Parties* choose an adjudicator jointly?

YES / NO

NEW ADJUDICATOR

93.2(2)
The chosen adjudicator becomes the *Adjudicator*

NOMINATED

93.2(2)
Either *Party* may ask the *Adjudicator nominating body* to choose an adjudicator

93.2(2)
The *Adjudicator nominating body* chooses an adjudicator within four days of the request

NOT LIABLE UNLESS ACTS IN BAD FAITH

93.2(3)
The *Adjudicator*, his employees and agents are not liable to the *Parties* for any action or failure to take action in an adjudication unless the action or failure to take action was in bad faith

ADJUDICATION

A
Sheet 2

Flow charts 93 and 94 Sheet 1 of 4
Dispute resolution

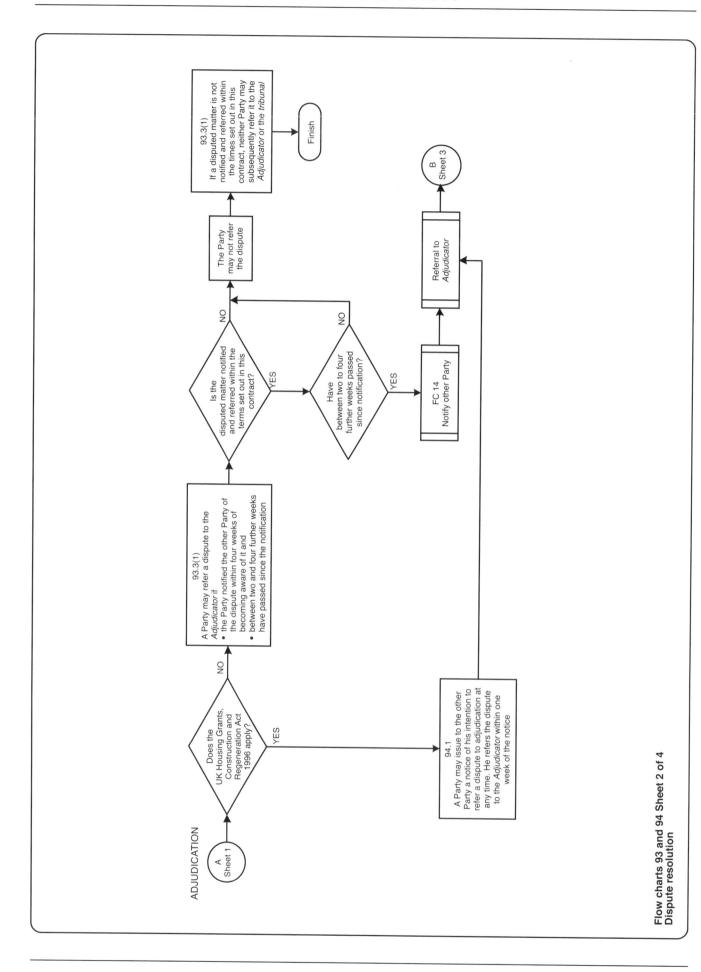
ADJUDICATION

A
Sheet 1

Does the UK Housing Grants, Construction and Regeneration Act 1996 apply?

NO →

93.3(1)
A Party may refer a dispute to the *Adjudicator* if
• the Party notified the other Party of the dispute within four weeks of becoming aware of it and
• between two and four further weeks have passed since the notification

→

Is the disputed matter notified and referred within the terms set out in this contract?

NO →

The Party may not refer the dispute

→

93.3(1)
If a disputed matter is not notified and referred within the times set out in this contract, neither Party may subsequently refer it to the *Adjudicator* or the *tribunal*

→ Finish

YES ↓

Have between two to four further weeks passed since notification?

NO →

YES →

FC 14
Notify other Party

→

Referral to *Adjudicator*

→ B
Sheet 3

YES (from first decision) →

94.1
A Party may issue to the other Party a notice of his intention to refer a dispute to adjudication at any time. He refers the dispute to the *Adjudicator* within one week of the notice

Flow charts 93 and 94 Sheet 2 of 4
Dispute resolution

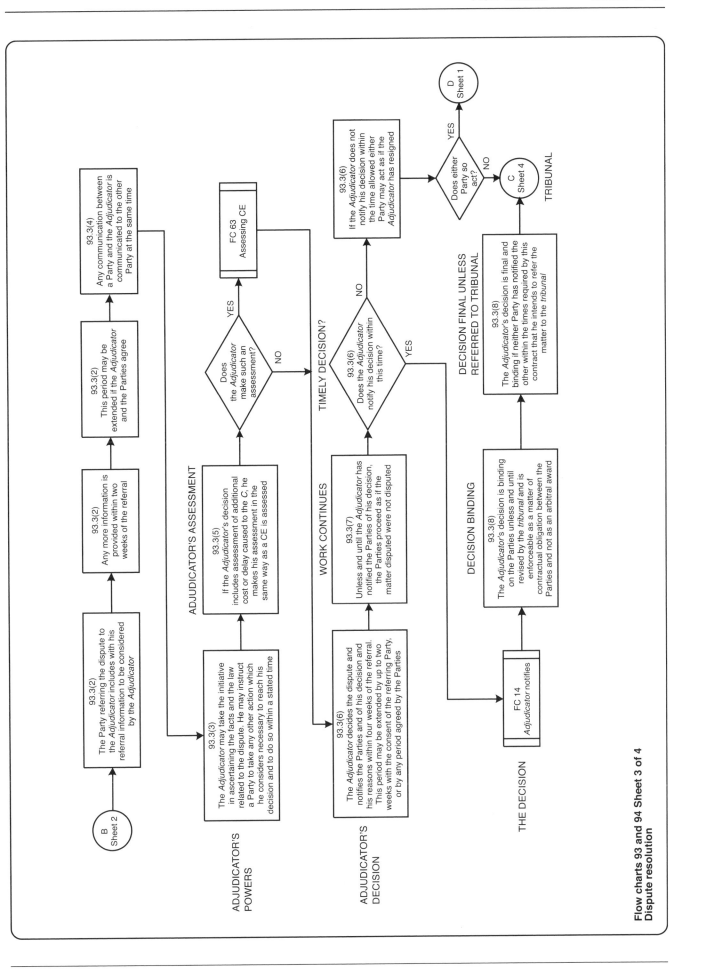

ADJUDICATOR'S POWERS

ADJUDICATOR'S ASSESSMENT

ADJUDICATOR'S DECISION

TIMELY DECISION?

WORK CONTINUES

THE DECISION

DECISION BINDING

DECISION FINAL UNLESS REFERRED TO TRIBUNAL

TRIBUNAL

93.3(2)
The Party referring the dispute to the *Adjudicator* includes with his referral information to be considered by the *Adjudicator*

93.3(2)
Any more information is provided within two weeks of the referral

93.3(2)
This period may be extended if the *Adjudicator* and the Parties agree

93.3(4)
Any communication between a Party and the *Adjudicator* is communicated to the other Party at the same time

93.3(3)
The *Adjudicator* may take the initiative in ascertaining the facts and the law related to the dispute. He may instruct a Party to take any other action which he considers necessary to reach his decision and to do so within a stated time

93.3(5)
If the *Adjudicator's* decision includes assessment of additional cost or delay caused to the *C*, he makes his assessment in the same way as a CE is assessed

Does the *Adjudicator* make such an assessment?

FC 63
Assessing CE

93.3(6)
The *Adjudicator* decides the dispute and notifies the Parties and of his decision and his reasons within four weeks of the referral. This period may be extended by up to two weeks with the consent of the referring Party, or by any period agreed by the Parties

93.3(7)
Unless and until the *Adjudicator* has notified the Parties of his decision, the Parties proceed as if the matter disputed were not disputed

93.3(6)
Does the *Adjudicator* notify his decision within this time?

93.3(6)
If the *Adjudicator* does not notify his decision within the time allowed either Party may act as if the *Adjudicator* has resigned

Does either Party so act?

93.3(8)
The *Adjudicator's* decision is binding on the Parties unless and until revised by the *tribunal* and is enforceable as a matter of contractual obligation between the Parties and not as an arbitral award

93.3(8)
The *Adjudicator's* decision is final and binding if neither Party has notified the other within the times required by this contract that he intends to refer the matter to the *tribunal*

FC 14
Adjudicator notifies

B
Sheet 2

D
Sheet 1

C
Sheet 4

YES

NO

YES

NO

YES

NO

Flow charts 93 and 94 Sheet 3 of 4
Dispute resolution

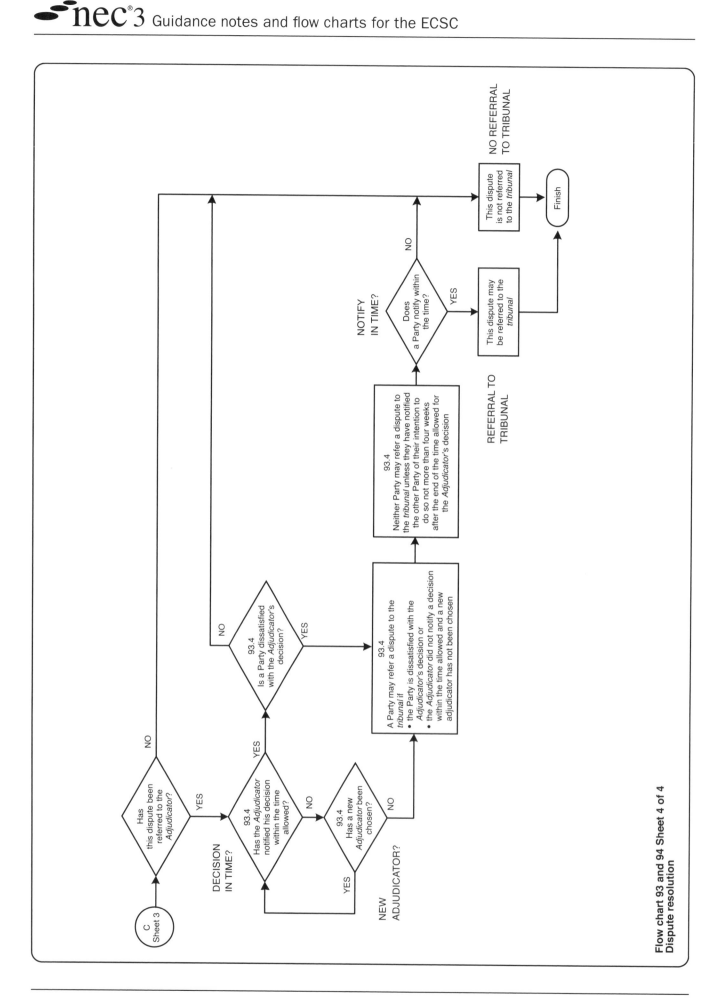

Flow chart 93 and 94 Sheet 4 of 4
Dispute resolution